Yasukuni Shrine

and the

Constraints on the Discourses of Nationalism

in Twentieth-Century Japan

by

Joshua Safier

ISBN: 0-9658564-1-0

DISSERTATION.COM

1997

Yasukuni Shrine

and the

Constraints on the Discourses of Nationalism

in Twentieth-Century Japan

by

Joshua Safier
B.A., Oberlin College, 1991

Submitted to the Department of East Asian Languages and Cultures and the Faculty of the Graduate School of the University of Kansas in partial fulfillment of the requirements for the degree of Master of Arts.

_____
Chairperson

_____
Committee Member

_____
Committee Member

_____
Committee Member

_____
Date, Thesis Accepted

Dedication

To Professor Ronald DiCenzo, the inspiration of my passion for Japan.

sensei, osewa ni narimashita

Abstract

The Yasukuni Shrine - - Japan's national memorial enshrining the spirits of Japanese soldiers killed in domestic and foreign wars - - occupies a peculiar chapter in Japanese history. Originally designed as a sanctuary to house the spirits of those who died in overthrowing the Tokugawa Regime, Yasukuni was nurtured by the state and then the military into a powerful religious and iconographic center to promote Japanese ultranationalism. Following the close of World War II, the Shrine became the subject of intense politico-religious debates as the Japanese, with the assistance of the international community, consigned themselves to the task of finding a place for Yasukuni as they worked on their postwar project of reinventing nationalism and cultural identity.

This thesis provides a narrative review of Yasukuni's history from its inception to the present, focusing on the critical years of 1985-1986, when Prime Minister Nakasone Yasuhiro sanctioned a commission to settle the Yasukuni problem. This study also represents one path in a quest toward a deeper understanding and definition of postwar Japanese nationalism and identity.

ii

Acknowledgments

In the research and writing of this project, I have benefited immensely from the knowledge, active interest, and support of many.

I would like to thank Professor William M. Tsutsui for his extensive, enthusiastic and sustained guidance and support. His erudition, forthrightness and keen constructive criticisms helped me to fine-tune this study from its inception.

I am also grateful to Professors Daniel Bays and Daniel Stevenson, who provided helpful suggestions and assistance; my good friend Chihiro Kawabata for sending essential source materials from Japan and expressing her views openly on issues related to this paper; my family, who have always supported me with the warmest love; and my mother, to whom I owe my ever-developing writing style and training.

My warmest words of gratitude are reserved for my wife, Elena. Her intellectual companionship, objective insights, and unswerving devotion were an invaluable necessity during the course of this study,

Table Of Contents

Introduction: Setting the Stage

On July 26, 1945, the Allied Powers issued the Potsdam Declaration which decreed that:

> The Japanese Government shall remove all obstacles to the revival and strengthening of democratic tendencies among the Japanese people. Freedom of speech, of religion, and of thought, as well as respect for the fundamental human rights, shall be established.[1]

This directive was explicitly designed to root out ultranationalism and militaristic notions of empire, and thus ensure a lasting peace in the world. In 1947, these democratic ideals were written into Japan's new Constitution by the American Occupation.

Moreover, in order to excise the heritage of expansionistic nationalism, MacArthur and his forces aimed directly to demobilize the Yasukuni Shrine as a government-sponsored religious institution. The physical edifice was allowed to remain standing, but the Shrine's control was removed from the auspices of the Imperial Army and Navy. Thus, the Shrine could only operate as a private religious organization. Whether or not the Japanese of the Cold War years welcomed and wholly accepted these new democratic principles was irrelevant at the time. In the wake of Japan's defeat, the vocation of survival, rather than

---

[1] *The Potsdam Declaration:* July 26, 1945, Paragraph 10, as cited in William P. Woodard, *The Allied Occupation of Japan 1945-1952 and Japanese Religions*. (Leiden, Netherlands: Brill, 1972), Appendix A. 1, p. 286.

the abstraction of nationalism was of paramount concern. In time, as Japan rose from the ashes, some Japanese began searching for the sense of cultural identity which lay buried amidst the rubble of war and suppressed by the victors' blueprint for peace.

In 1952, after the American Occupation had left Japan, right-wing groups and members of the *Nihon Izokukai* (The Japan's Bereaved Families Association) launched a movement to rehabilitate the Yasukuni Shrine as a government-sponsored institution.[2] These political drives were severely criticized by leftist parties, labor unions, and various religious organizations because they violated Articles 20 and 89 of Japan's new Constitution. Article 20 guarantees the freedom of religion and the separation of religion and state; and Article 89 forbids the use of public funds for religious purposes. Not only did constitutional law prohibit state patronage of the Yasukuni Shrine, but the national and international climate of the times looked with disdain and distrust upon every movement which sought to renew a sense of nationalism in Japan.

---

[2] *Originally established in 1947 as the Nihon Izoku Kosei Renmei (Bereaved Families Welfare Alliance), the Nihon Izokukai has become one of Japan's most powerful and tightly organized political pressure groups. It was founded to force the postwar government to honor the prewar government's commitment to provide military pensions for the families of the war dead. Since 1952, it has become an active group supporting the re-nationalization of Yasukuni Shrine. Hiroshi Ueda, "Yasukuni Shrine Reform Remains Hot Live Issue," Japan Times Weekly, May 11, 1974; Oe Shinobu, Yasukuni Jinja mondai, (Tokyo, Iwanami Shoten, 1984), p. 12.*

Nevertheless, since the early 1960s, the Liberal Democratic Party (LDP) and the *Nihon Izokukai* steadily increased their activities to re-establish state patronage of the Shrine by submitting formal bills for its adoption to the Diet. All of these proposals were defeated, sending a powerful message to LDP members and their constituents that Yasukuni should rightfully remain within the guidelines of the Constitution.

The LDP's struggle to re-legitimize Yasukuni as a national institution highlighted the fact that Japan's postwar search for national identity hinged not only on building a new sense of nationalism, but also on escaping the memory of their previous one. Every year, on and around August 15, global attention shifts toward Japan's commemoration of the end of World War II. During this time, a wave of media scrutiny recalls Yasukuni's prewar role, including its association with the Emperor and its manipulation by the military elite. In this way, the image of Yasukuni as a politically charged religious institution, dedicated solely to memorializing the war dead and expressing patriotic sentiments, is annually revitalized in the public imagination. Consequently, the Shrine's aura as a symbol of aggression, ethnocentrism, emperor-ism, and religious fanaticism reminiscent of Japan's prewar personality is regularly reinforced.

Moreover, the international community watches with critical eyes as the annual period of protest over the incumbent Japanese Prime Minister's decision to visit the Shrine begins. If he pays an official visit to Yasukuni, then Japan is violating constitutional law, the spirit of democracy, and is returning to prewar methods of rule. If the Prime Minister does *not* visit, then the conservative right and approximately 4.5 million members of the *Nihon Izokukai* demand to know why Japanese leaders are betraying their own cultural history. Even though Yasukuni was ideologically deadened in 1945, its prewar symbolism and psychological impact on the world remains frozen in time. Its origin, history and national significance have left an indelible impression upon world memory and this image has contributed to the complexity of the Yasukuni controversy.

On August 15, 1985, the LDP changed its tactics when Nakasone Yasuhiro became the first government dignitary since World War II to visit the Yasukuni Shrine and to sign the visitor's book in his official capacity as Prime Minister. His offering to the shrine, an expensive sprig from a sacred tree, was reimbursed from the public purse.[3] The reverberations of this event still echo in public memory.[4] Over the past decade, the media, intellectuals, statesmen,

---

[3] *"Nakasone Visits Yasukuni Ignoring Religious Groups," The Japan Times*, 16 August 1984, p. 203.

[4] *By public memory, I am referring to one specific narrative of history that has been sewn together by several informants. First, the general public's individual and collective historical experiences. That is, their consumption, processing and reflection of historical events as they relate to them and their particular station in society at both the time the event(s) occurred as well as past recollection(s) of the event. Secondly, members of the state and academicians who, through public expression, display and written format, inform the general public about vantage points and perspectives from*

4

various organized religious groups, pacifists, leftists, the governments of South Korea and China, and Southeast Asian countries subjected to Japanese exploitation during World War II, have vocally expressed their outrage and adamantly protested the possible re-nationalization of the Yasukuni Shrine through such official and religious displays of support.

But where does one place the Yasukuni Shrine in postwar Japan? Why does the shrine continue to draw worldwide attention if it is constitutionally

---

which to view specific issues and events. Textbooks, for example, represent one powerful channel through which public memory is informed and directed. In Japan's case, the Monbusho's (Ministry of Education) editing of Japan's role during World War II, specifically the omission of war atrocities, has served to formulate and instill a specific version of the war within the minds of younger generations of Japanese.

Thirdly, public memory is created by the media, including newspapers and news broadcasts that reach a wide and diverse audience. These three taxonomies are by no means exhaustive, but they represent the more prevalent architects of public memory.

In reference to international public memory, specifically in the case of Yasukuni, the public memories of many nations exploited by Japanese wartime aggression have converged to achieve a consensus on what global memory surrounding Yasukuni should entail. Regardless of the fact that these nations (China, Korea, Southeast Asian countries, United States, Britain, etc. . .) possess a different perspective of World War II and have processed those events according to cultural specific variants, each nation has formulated the same general opinion that Yasukuni is a symbol of Japanese militarism. This memory (based upon historical recollection) has been kept alive for 41 years by the masses, politicians, academicians, and media all over the world. No one group is responsible for writing public memory alone. Instead, each group interacts concomitantly with one another forming a discourse and ongoing dialectic bent on experience, perception, perspective, hearsay and fiction.

Finally, using Yasukuni once again as the modus operandi, Japan's national public memory of Yasukuni has been subjugated to that of international memory. In other words, it does not matter if Japanese officials try to cleanse their histories, cloak their visits in unofficial garb or political jargon, or assert that Yasukuni is a national memorial and deserves the patronage of the state. Yasukuni has been branded globally and that has remained the dominant recollection.

My understanding and interpolation of public memory draws in part from Carol Gluck's lectures on "Master Narratives and Epochal Moments in Modern Japanese History," (1996) and also Gluck's, "The Past in the Present," in Andrew Gordon's, Postwar Japan as History, Berkeley: University of California Press, 1993, pp. 64-95.

forbidden to be patronized by the state or to act as a medium through which state policy is disseminated? Why have prominent statesmen in postwar Japan continually looked to this particular shrine as a source of national unity? Is it an attempt to thwart potentially revolutionary aspects of democracy and postwar social change as Helen Hardacre suggests in Shinto and the State?

> Another goal [of the Japanese government to revive the symbolism of Shinto] is the creation of a compelling myth of cultural identity encompassing a formula for the legitimation of the state, one that will again submerge the divisions of gender, class, and ethnicity in the cozy, penumbral illusion of spiritual unity, articulated in the characteristically vague and incontrovertible rites and symbols of Shinto, with special use of the Yasukuni Shrine.[5]

Or, more to the point, is the Japanese government renewing its historical manipulation of religious institutions for the purposes of political indoctrination and ideological construction?

The aim of this study is to re-evaluate the nature of postwar Japanese nationalism through the prism of the ongoing controversy over the Yasukuni Shrine. In order to establish Yasukuni as one of the centers where postwar nationalism is being debated and fashioned, this work will outline Yasukuni's history in the context of postwar political and cultural change, and analyze a report drafted in 1984 by an officially appointed Japanese advisory commission. Appraising the report will involve delineating three schools of thought,

---

[5] Hardacre, Helen. *Shinto and the State: 1868-1988*. Princeton: Princeton University Press, 1989, p. 9.

establishing the credibility of the commission members to validate their arguments, and exploring the reasons why a consensus could not be reached. Having assessed the state of the debate, this work will seek to gauge Yasukuni's potency as a symbol in the postwar era and reflect on the nature of Japanese nationalism. It is my contention that the message and mission of prewar Japanese nationalism was not obliterated by an American-imposed Constitution, but persists today, intertwined with the new ideological imperatives of "internationalization" (*kokusaika*).

This study is divided into four chapters that progress forward chronologically. The first chapter presents an historical overview of the Yasukuni Shrine between 1869 and 1945. Originally established as a monument to the loyalists who sacrificed their lives for the restoration of the Emperor and the overthrow of the Tokugawa Bakufu, Yasukuni was steadily transformed into a politico-religious tool for enhancing the authority of the ruling Meiji elite, and later, for supporting the Ministry of War's expansionist policies. Under the auspices of the Meiji government and the Ministry of War, the Shrine was intimately connected with the divinity of the Emperor and shrouded in religious ceremony. This became part of the powerful ideological apparatus wielded by the military to manipulate the country toward war.

Chapter Two surveys the Shrine's history from 1945 through 1984 by examining the demobilization of Yasukuni by SCAP (Supreme Commander for the Allied Powers) and the subsequent measures taken by the *Nihon Izokukai* and elements in the Liberal Democratic Party to revitalize state patronage of Yasukuni. In the wake of war, defeat and occupation, a rising sense of concern over the future of Japanese identity emerged within Japan. To address this lingering problem, reinvigorate Japanese nationalism, and dispel a taboo subject in national affairs, Prime Minister Nakasone presented his "New Vision" of Japan and placed the Yasukuni Shrine at the iconographic center of Japan's new nationalism. This conservative tactic had far reaching domestic and international implications. Nakasone ignited a national debate between conservative and progressive factions by revitalizing traditional values and masking his Japan-centric intentions behind the facade of Japanese internationalization. Internationally, foreign criticism and suspicion applied continuous pressure to the realm of Japan's external relations.

Nakasone was convinced that an international Japan rested on a strong sense of national self-confidence created through economic and technological prowess. He believed Yasukuni represented a formidable cultural center capable of redirecting Japan's energies and harnessing these powers to lead the nation into the twenty-first century. One way in which Nakasone tried to bridge "traditional reverence" for the war dead (and, by extension, traditional values) with a more forward-looking nationalism was to sanction a commission to study and achieve a consensus on the Yasukuni issue.

Chapter Three analyzes the results of that inquiry which were submitted in a written report to the Diet on August 9, 1985. This section outlines the predominant factors contributing to the commission's establishment and introduces the commission members and their respective political leanings. I will discuss the major issues debated during the commission's twenty-one meetings, and gauge public reactions to their final report from relevant Japanese newspapers of the time. Three schools of thought are clearly presented in that report, suggesting the pluralistic political climate that had emerged in postwar Japan. As I will show, the commission's report demonstrates both how and why the Yasukuni controversy has remained paralyzed for so long. The report further suggests the diffuse nature of postwar Japanese nationalism.

In the final chapter, an evaluation of the Yasukuni Shrine controversy is presented from two perspectives: its potency as a symbol of nationalism in postwar Japan and its blending with the new ideological requisites of internationalization (*kokusaika*). Whereas previous studies have emphasized an evolving "new nationalism" in postwar Japan, excluding traditional symbols of nationalism and the ideology they stood for, this section suggests that the message and mission of prewar Japanese nationalism has been, to a certain extent, incorporated into the postwar ideological landscape through cloaking it in the guise of internationalization.

In the course of researching this topic, several limitations arose which were addressed as follows. The general framework of this thesis provides a narrative history of the Yasukuni Shrine between 1869 and 1996. Due to the absence of any comprehensive historical survey of Yasukuni in English, I have pieced together an historical picture of the shrine from both English and Japanese sources.

Throughout this study, every effort has been made to translate selected Japanese sources with the utmost accuracy. Any shortcomings are clearly the fault of this author. The major primary source for this project is the commission's official report printed in the 1985 issue of *Jurisuto*. Since the report consists of the anonymous opinions of fifteen commission members, linking any findings to specific members was virtually impossible. Nevertheless, I have tried to compensate for this in two ways. First, I have utilized several germane commentaries accompanying the report which have been written by the same commission members or pertinent members of Japan's intelligentsia. These commentaries served to illuminate related issues and made deciphering the political leanings of the members slightly less ambiguous. Secondly, I have

10

included biographical sketches on all fifteen members in a separate appendix.[6]

A final point regarding nomenclature is in order. Prime Minister Nakasone was fond of establishing advisory panels to boost his personal political agenda. Although this particular advisory council has been formally called the "LDP Subcommittee on the Yasukuni Shrine Issue,"[7] I will refer to this commission as the Hayashi Commission, after its Chairman, Hayashi Keizo.

Definitions: Nationalism and the Ideological Process

As one of the most potent forces at work in the modern world, nationalism has been rigorously studied by political scientists, historians and economists. Each group has fashioned its own definition(s) of nationalism while remaining within its own field(s) of expertise. While many comparative studies have been undertaken, the trend has been not to stray beyond one's discipline. According to the political scientist Hans Kohn, nationalism is an historical phenomenon characterized by a sense of pride and patriotism. It is a product of group loyalty and shared consciousness resulting in a strong feeling of national identity and

---

[6]   The major source for this information was the _Gendai Nihon shippitsusha daijiten_ 77/84 (Biographical Dictionary of Modern Japan). Tokyo: Nichigai Associates, 1984-85.

[7]   "Official Yasukuni Visits Discussed by LDP Body," _The Japan Times_, July 22, 1983.

cultural uniqueness.[8]   Historian Delmer Brown, meanwhile, has described

nationalism as an "intellectual and emotional phenomenon," one that does not

"become a significant socio-psychological force until the elements [shared

cultural possessions, experiences, ideas, beliefs, hopes, and fears] have been

activated by social and intellectual developments which place the members of a

nation into a close interdependent relationship."[9]   These broader definitions

allow for a greater understanding of nationalism and its development at different

levels of society and at different historical moments.

Although these definitions can be applied internationally, other factors

such as geographical location, ethnic diversity, and cultural specificity seep into

the formula and can give rise to variations. In an effort to avoid such pitfalls and

to allow Japan's unique variation of nationalism to emerge, I have chosen a

general definition with which to work.   According to the International

Encyclopedia of the Social Sciences:

> Nationalism is a political creed that underlies the cohesion of
> modern societies and legitimizes their claim to authority.
> Nationalism centers the supreme loyalty of the overwhelming
> majority of the people upon the nation-state, either existing or

---

[8]   Kohn, Hans. *Nationalism: Its Meaning and History*. Princeton:
D. Van Nostrand Company, INC., 1955, p. 9.

[9]   Brown, Delmer M.   *Nationalism in Japan: An Introductory Historical
Analysis*. Berkeley: University of California Press, 1955, p. 2.

12

desired. The nation-state is regarded not only as the ideal, "natural," or "normal" form of political organization but also as the indispensable framework for all social, cultural and economic activities.[10]

The reasons why nationalism emerges are as diverse as its definitions.

In his essay, "Some Recent Approaches to Japanese Nationalism," historian Kenneth Pyle delineates at least six distinct approaches to the development of this phenomenon. For example, nationalism can be the product of cultural disorientation or disruption resulting from interaction with outside cultures; it can be wielded as an ideological weapon by the ruling elite to further its own social class; it can also be an outlet for social duress induced by rapid social change or the uneven pace of development between different social groups or regions.[11]

These genealogies may help clarify the external manifestations nationalism can assume, but they do not sufficiently explain the internal mechanisms at work.

Since nationalism will be treated as a form of ideology in this study, some understanding of the theoretical underpinnings of nationalism deserve attention.

One of the current trends in Japanese historiography is analyzing the

---

[10]   *The International Encyclopedia of the Social Sciences.* David L. Sills, ed. *International Encyclopedia of the Social Sciences* (New York: 1968), s. v. "Nationalism," by Hans Kohn.

[11]   Pyle, Kenneth. "A Symposium on Japanese Nationalism: Some Recent Approaches to Japanese Nationalism." *Journal of Asian Studies*, vol. 31, no. 5 (1971): 5-16.

13

creation of ideology in modern Japan. In other words, scholars are examining ideology as an idea or set of ideas that provide a consistent intellectual framework for viewing the past and experiencing the present, rather than considering history to be a *natural* unfolding of events. Although explained below in theoretical terms, the connection between the construction of ideology and the evolution of the Yasukuni Shrine as a pivotal symbol of nationalism in Japan's pre- and postwar ideological process will be elucidated in succeeding chapters.

In its most conventional sense, ideology constrains or subjects people to a specific socio-political order through shared beliefs, values and ideas.[12] In addition, there must always be two active agents involved: the inventors, those who create and promote the ideology, and, the recipients, those who accept it. For the inventors, ideology serves as a means of rationalizing their rule by disguising it as the natural state of things.[13] As for the recipients, we must accept that they subscribe, willingly or unwillingly, consciously or unconsciously, to the ideas being prescribed.

A case in point is the ingenuity with which the Meiji oligarchy, and later

---

[12]   Vlastos, Steven. *Peasant Protests and Uprisings in Tokugawa Japan*. Berkeley: The University of California Press, 1986, p. 15.

[13]   John Goodman and Kirsten Refsing. *Ideology and Practice in Modern Japan*. New York: Routledge, 1992, p. 11.

the Ministry of War, constructed prewar Japanese ideology (1868-1945). Their genius rested in their ability to create what Prasenjit Duara has coined a "narrative of descent," whereby the present was re-invented by re-connecting it to the past.[14] In effect, a new history emerged, one that appeared genuine because it successfully grafted tradition to the modern. History appeared to the public as continuous and progressive, but it was also dually designed to legitimate the ideology being professed and, for our purposes, ignite the flames of nationalism.

In Japan's case, this historical transformation was realized by merging traditional values and institutions into the present, thus fashioning a continuous historical narrative in the popular imagination. The Meiji leaders were able to combine myth derived from the past (the Emperor's divinity through his association with an unbroken Imperial line) with national reform and progress (modernization) to the extent that both were imagined by the Japanese to co-exist as one entity. Through ideological channels such as schools and national memorials, like Yasukuni, the government artificially aroused the Japanese populace and transformed the country into a nationalistic state. From this perspective, prewar ideology can be characterized as a political deception pulled

---

[14] Duara, Prasenjit. *Rescuing History from the Nation.* Chicago: The University of Chicago Press, 1995, p. 81.

over the *free* consciousness of the Japanese people. The Japanese were coerced into believing the myth of the Emperor ideology and envisioned their country's reality according to the rhetorical strategies of the ruling elite.

But ideology is not merely a product of false consciousness or a propagandisitc deception pulled over the hearts and minds of the people. This definition seems to exclude the recipients from what is clearly a collective enterprise. In order for ideology to take root there must exist a sense of cooperation between the rulers and the ruled. To help increase our field of vision in understanding the fuller implications of ideology, it will prove helpful to briefly examine several approaches found within the range of theoretical possibilities.

Within any society there is a multiplicity of ideologies, each of which has its own values and meanings. But what gives one ideology dominance over the others? Carol Gluck suggests that an ideology becomes orthodoxy when a particular set of ideas receives the majority of consent of the population. Ideological domination is contingent upon the depth to which these ideas have permeated the social consciousness. Citing Gramsci's conception of ideological hegemony, Gluck states:

> . . . when a social group is successful in persuading others of the validity of its own world view, force does not greatly exceed

consent. The consent, moreover, so penetrates the society that to many it seems commonsensical, natural, and at times invisible.[15]

We must accept the fact that ideology, while at some point a new behavior to be learned, disappears from conscious thought only to be adhered to naturally. Indeed, as Maruyama Masao asserts, rulers will rule only if their brand of ideology is capable of casting an invisible net over the populace.[16]

Conversely, ideologies which become visible, or which loosen their mental and spiritual hold on the populace due to changing historical events, can allow for the emergence of new sets of ideas among the people. In other words, people may once again select from among new sets of ideas being propagated or created and conduct their lives accordingly.

To help clarify this line of thought, consider how the Meiji ideologues were capable of distancing or removing themselves from the waning (yet deeply embedded) Tokugawa system of thought control that guided their everyday lives. The emergence of the Meiji intelligentsia was due, in part, to their ability to escape one ideological "net" and begin the construction and casting of another. This was accomplished by exposing, or consciously recognizing the weakened state of Tokugawa thought control and beginning the dissemination of a new set

---

[15]   Gluck, Carol. *Japan's Modern Myths: Ideology in the Late Meiji Period*. Princeton: Princeton University Press, 1985, p. 7.

[16]   Irokawa, Daikichi. *The Culture of the Meiji Period*. Princeton: Princeton

of ideas, such as the Emperor ideology. The debilitated state of the Tokugawa shogunate, together with its ineptness in dealing with the encroachment of foreign countries, provided fertile ground for a new ideology bent on national reform and modernization. Whether or not ideological change was a result of *natural* historical timing, it seems fair to conclude that prewar Japanese ideology (Emperor Ideology) enveloped the nation because it promised a new era and an enlightened stage of civilization that steadily progressed toward modernization. As will be demonstrated below, the Emperor ideology was powerful enough to confront the onslaught of Western imperialism and insure the survival of the modern Japanese nation-state.

With this in mind, we can invite another definition of ideology into this theoretical picture. According to Victor Koschmann,

> Ideologies not only subject people to a given order. They also qualify them for conscious social action, including actions of gradual or revolutionary change. Ideologies do not function merely as "social cement."[17]

In this sense, once ideologies gain public support and begin the construction of daily realities, people can be persuaded to act according to specific ideas on their own accord. They consciously make a choice to abide by rules and support

---

University Press, 1985, p. 271.

[17]   *Koschmann, Victor. The Mito Ideology: Discourse, Reform and Insurrection in Late Tokugawa Japan, 1790-1864. Berkeley: The University of California Press, 1987, p. 7.*

18

a specific societal order by unconsciously submitting to a system of ideas. This of course hinges on the presumption that these rules have become invisible, or part of the greater social unconscious. The word "persuaded" as used above may harbor negative connotations, but consent on the recipient's part still shows acceptance of the ideology.[18] Ideological acceptance has the dual effect of publically legitimizing the ruling faction and cloaking what is actually a ruler-and-ruled relationship as one built on equality and consensus.

The lines of demarcation between nationalism and ideology as I have described them may seem rather obscure, but this is because they appear to this author as one and the same when analyzing the machinery of prewar Japanese nationalism. Nationalism, as an ideology, was the crucial ingredient necessary to unite Japan and carry her successfully through the transition from a feudal state to one of modernization. Prewar Japanese nationalism was founded on a formula consisting of traditional ethics, modern statecraft, and a touch of fiction. As Gluck has suggested, the Emperor, Yasukuni, and the education system were all contributing agents to nationalism. As prewar Japan's primary ideology,

---

[18]   *Kenneth Pyle identifies six distinct approaches to nationalism and how it is developed. According to what he coins the "interest theory," the ruling elite will wield nationalist doctrine as an ideological weapon to further the interest of its own social class. This theory is heavily influenced by the principles of Marxism and pertains to negative images which may arise over actions motivated through self-interest. Kenneth Pyle. "A Symposium on Japanese Nationalism: Some Recent Approaches to Japanese Nationalism." Journal of Asian Studies, vol. 31, no. 5 (1971): pp. 5-16.*

nationalism provided a cure for Japan's domestic and international ills.

The Yasukuni Shrine has been chosen for this study as one locus among many from which to view Japan's past, experience its present, and speculate on its future. The task of synthesizing the nature of ideology and the role of Yasukuni in perpetuating nationalism occupies the pages of the following chapters.

Chapter I   Yasukuni: A Historical Overview, 1869-1945

Today, as in June of 1869, the Yasukuni Shrine stands on the top of Kudan Hill northeast of the Imperial Palace. Rising majestically before a white gravel path leading to the main shrine is a *torii*, a traditional Japanese symbol representing sacred space. Within the compound, two large wooden buildings, a *Honden* (Main Shrine) and a *Haiden* (Hall of Worship) are roofed in copper, surrounded by a wide rectangular veranda, and connected by an open corridor. One might be tempted to conclude, as at least one writer has, that Yasukuni's appearance represents the essence of peace.[19] It is a place that tempts the pedestrian to escape the hustle of inner-city Tokyo life. However, within the Shrine's precincts, cherry trees bearing white tags with the names of Imperial Army Regiments and famous battleships contrast sharply with the sanctuary's external appearance of a shrine dedicated to the promulgation of peace.[20]

The Yasukuni Shrine represents a peculiar concept of peace, one that is shrouded in over fifty years of an even more peculiar controversy, obscuring, in

---

[19]   Sawafuji, Toichiro. *Iwate Yasukuni iken sosho*, *(Opinion on the Lawsuit between Yasukuni and Iwate Prefecture)*, *Shin Nihon Shuppansha, 1992, p. 158.*

[20]   Buruma, Ian. *The Wages of Guilt: Memories of War in Germany and Japan*. *New York: Harper Collins, 1994, p. 221.*

21

some ways, more than it explains about modern Japanese nationalism.[21] The contemporary images painted above describe a national symbol which many Japanese find difficult to speak about because it reflects a dark period of their country's history. For many younger Japanese, their knowledge of the Shrine is dominated by political debates and international recriminations, resulting in confusion or indifference. To gain a greater understanding of the role the Yasukuni Shrine plays in contemporary Japan, it is necessary to recount its long and evocative past, and to trace the evolution of Yasukuni from a symbol of patriotism to an international symbol of aggression.

*   *   *

In the waning years of the Tokugawa shogunate, while the civil war between the Imperial loyalists and Tokugawa forces spiraled toward the Meiji Restoration, the first recorded Shinto ceremony honoring the war dead took place. In December of 1862, sixty members of the loyalist Tsuwano clan gathered in Kyoto to hold a *shokonsai*, or "spirit - inviting - rite" at the *Reimeisha*, a Shinto funeral hall on Higashiyama. This Shinto ceremony commemorated the spirits of comrades who had died in battle for the loyalist cause since 1858. In 1863, a similar ceremony was observed within the precincts of the Gion Shrine (also in Kyoto), and a small shrine-like structure called a *shokonsha* -- possibly

---

[21] Chapman, William. *Inventing Japan: The Making of a Postwar Civilization*. New York: Prentice Hall Press, 1991, p. 231.

the first spirit invoking shrine -- was erected for the occasion; but it had to be immediately destroyed for fear of detection by the shogun's spies.[22]

The primary impetus for these ceremonies grew out of respect for fallen comrades and human compassion. They were also a reflection of Restoration Shinto. During the Tokugawa period, the dead had been buried according to Buddhist ritual. However, to leaders of the restoration movement, Buddhism was perceived as a corrupting foreign influence incompatible with the Japanese spirit.[23] To loyalist leaders dependent upon military support from commoners and *samurai*, the Shinto ritual provided them with an indigenous ideological tool to mobilize patriotic sentiments. Used as a means of encouraging dedication and sacrifice to the loyalist cause, *shokonsha* became the physical symbols of group integration, and the accompanying rituals played an instrumental psychological and cultural role in bolstering a sense of patriotism.[24]

At about the same time, other similar shrines consoling the spirits of the war dead began cropping up in domains that were loyal to the imperial cause. In 1864, thirty-seven shrines were built (of which eighteen were in Yamaguchi) and

---

[22] Woodard, William. "Yasukuni Shrine," *Japan Christian Quarterly*. 37 (Spring 1971): 72-79.

[23] Kitagawa, Joseph M. *Religion in Japanese History*. New York: Columbia University press, 1990, p. 203. and, Woodard, Yasukuni Shrine," p. 76.

[24] Goodman and Refsing, *Ideology and Practice in Modern Japan*, p. 26.

2,016 comrades were deified.[25] Official ceremonies honoring the war dead continued in Kyoto until the loyalists succeeded in overthrowing the Tokugawa shogunate in 1868. An Eastern Expeditionary Force composed of loyalist troops entered Edo Castle on April 21, 1868. On June 2 of the same year, a spirit-invoking ceremony in honor of those who lost their lives in this campaign against Tokugawa forces at Edo Castle was observed. Subsequently, this particular ceremony came to be regarded as the origin of the Yasukuni Shrine which, in the beginning, was called the Tokyo *Shokonsha*.[26]

By 1876, some 105 shrines had been dedicated to the spirits of 6,733 loyalist soldiers.[27] In many cases, these shrines received funding from the state. According to Hardacre's research on government expenditures for religious institutions, Shinto shrines deemed to be of significant national and Imperial importance regularly received state appropriations. Between 1902 and 1944, annual state appropriations for the Imperial Grand Shrines at Ise steadily increased from 50,000 yen to 230,000 yen. State funds were granted to specific shrines damaged or destroyed by fire or other natural disasters. The Yasukuni

---

[25]   *Yamaguchi is the Western-most prefecture on the island of Honshu. The large number of shrines may be related to the fact that many loyalists came from this particular region (Choshu), and because it was the furthest distance from the capital, where the Tokugawa Shogun resided.*

[26]   *Woodard, "Yasukuni Shrine," p. 76.*

[27]   *Woodard, "Yasukuni Shrine," p. 76.*

24

Shrine annually received funds from the Ministry of the Army, and shrines constructed at state initiative, such as the Meiji Shrine, were also supported by the state.[28] The increase in shrines and funding indicates a growing concern among the people for formal commemoration ceremonies and an increasing desire on the part of loyalist leaders to sanction national sentiment and solidarity. In 1879, after the seat of the new Meiji government had been transferred from Kyoto to Tokyo and the ideological potency of the shrine recognized, its name was changed to *Yasukuni Jinja* (shrine) and it was classified as a Special Government Shrine (*bekkaku kampeisha*).[29]

The name of the shrine further suggested its national significance. In its constituent parts *Yasu* means "peace(ful)," and *kuni* is "country." Therefore, Yasukuni Shrine came to symbolize a peaceful nation brought about after years of internal strife through the ultimate sacrifices made by fellow countrymen.

*   *   *

From the moment the Meiji oligarchs came to power they were confronted with a vexing dilemma. On the one hand, they recognized that modernizing the nation to escape potential Western colonization was imperative.

---

[28]   Hardacre, *Shinto and the State*, p. 166.

[29]   Woodard, "Yasukuni Shrine," p. 76.

However, they were also cognizant of the potential danger that economic development would be accompanied by widespread social disruption. The Meiji leaders were well aware of the social consequences accompanying industrialization in other nations, and expected the process to spark similar tensions in Japan. To counter these adverse effects, the Meiji government invented an elaborate series of imperial myths around the Emperor, instilling within the Japanese what Japanese scholars have called the, *tennosei ideorogii*, or the ideology of the emperor system. Gluck suggests that the heyday of the *tennosei* ideology stretched from 1890, when the Meiji constitution established the new political structures of modern Japan, to 1945, when these structures collapsed with Japan's surrender.[30]

The emperor system has been analyzed by many scholars. Gluck argues that the ideological landscape of the Meiji period "emphasized diversity, not consensus," and that the emperor ideology represented only one powerful agent among many responsible for the spiritual and patriotic mobilization of the Japanese.[31] Others, such as Irokawa Daikichi, have suggested that the emperor ideology was an all consuming force, an "illusion" encompassing the

---

[30]   *Gluck, Japan's Modern Myths, p. 5.*

[31]   *Gluck, Japan's Modern Myths, p. 15.*

26

"entire constellation of political, economic, and educational policies by which the government undertook to rule the people."[32] The emperor ideology was a spiritual phenomenon which helps to explain why it captured the public imagination so intensely. Both Gluck and Irokawa agree that the emperor system became part of everyday reality to the people of prewar Japan. According to Irokawa:

> The emperor system as a way of thinking was like an enormous black box into which the whole nation, intellectuals as well as commoners, unknowingly walked. Once within its confines, the corners of the box obscured in the darkness, the people were unable to see what it was that hemmed them in. The emperor system became part of the landscape, disappearing into the Japanese environment until the people thought it was a product of their own village community, rather than a system of control from above.[33]

Since the illusion, or *myth*, portrayed the emperor as a figure associated with an unbroken and divine lineage, bestowing upon him an aura of timelessness, the Meiji government could claim their ideology existed from the beginning of time. Moreover, the emperor became the crucial component in what Kenneth Pyle has termed the "technology of nationalism" because the emperor represented an easily understood link between the present and the

---

[32] Irokawa Daikichi. *The Culture of the Meiji Period*. Princeton: Princeton University Press, 1985, p. 245.

[33] Irokawa, *The Culture of the Meiji Period*, p. 245-246.

past.[34] Throughout the Meiji period, intellectuals and bureaucrats worked adamantly to counter the adverse effects of modernization. Through experimentation with a variety of laws, institutions, ideologies, and policies designed to ameliorate class conflict, absorb new groups into the political process, and promote loyalty to the regime, the Meiji leaders gradually perfected the *technology* of Japanese nationalism.[35] In this way, the Meiji government could ensure maximum support from the more traditional rural sectors of the population who were most likely to feel alienated by the government's agenda for modernization. The emperor system thus secured the peripheral and rural regions of Japan to the center.

Pulsing at the core of this apparatus was the much discussed concept of *kokutai*, described by Irokawa as an "amorphous spiritual force" that could be summoned in times of national crisis to prepare the nation and unite the people. *Kokutai* was a "moral concept that constituted the very essence of the state," fusing the emperor and his inviolability with the popular mind through education, politics and social values.[36] The emperor ideology's value system was

---

[34] Pyle, Kenneth. *"The Technology of Japanese Nationalism: The Local Improvement Movement, 1900-1918," Journal of Asian Studies. 33, no. 1 (1973): 51-65.*

[35] Pyle, *"The Technology of Nationalism," p. 5.*

[36] Irokawa, *The Culture of the Meiji period, pp. 245-311.*

predicated upon the people's unconditional and unlimited responsibility for protecting this system and the sacredness of the emperor, who was portrayed as the central authoritative figure and adherent of the Japanese people and national polity.

To enhance its effect, national memorials represented another avenue for stimulating and mobilizing Japanese nationalism. As a physical expression of the Meiji government's will, Yasukuni became one of many symbolic muscles through which the government flexed its new ideological agenda. The Shrine was conveniently expropriated as a tool to sway public opinion and instill traditional values, and it performed flawlessly as a "conduit through which the emperor ideology passed virtually unimpeded to its intended audience."[37] In 1868, the Meiji government announced that Yasukuni was ranked second only to the Grand Shrine at Ise and had a special relationship to the Imperial family. Therefore, Yasukuni was originally used to legitimize the fledgling Meiji government by forging associations between the state and the imperial family, as well as the spiritual realm.

An Imperial Rescript promulgated in the spring of 1868 articulated this connection explicitly, honoring those who gave their lives against the Tokugawa Shoguate:

---

[37]   Gluck, _Japan's Modern Myths_, p. 12.

29

They lost their lives because of their faithfulness to the principle of loyalty and patriotism and also because of their leadership in the movement started for the cause of Tenno. They had no energy left to spare for the cause of their parents, they deserted their homes, relinquishing their feudal fiefs, they found themselves refugees in strange corners of this land, they were homeless wanderers throughout this land where they once had homes, they underwent hardships of all descriptions . . . . They did this only to bring every member of the nation to the knowledge of those noble principles of which they should be considered observant. They were actuated by their earnest sincerity to undertake the restoration of the Throne to its old prestige, dignity, and sovereign power. They must be accorded justice with due honor; their noble achievements should be properly repaid. Those who render valuable services with silent efforts and whose achievements constituted a cause of the increase of national prosperity and the enhancement of the Imperial fortunes, must not be left to remain in obscurity.[38]

The Shrine's supposed religious purpose was to provide a sanctuary where the Emperor conducted rituals over the spirits of the war dead who sacrificed themselves for his honor and glory. Regardless of their earthly stations, soldiers enshrined at Yasukuni were apotheosized (*goshi*) and worshipped as *kami*, or dieties safeguarding the nation, by the Emperor himself.[39] The ultimate sacrifice, loyalty and patriotism was thus displayed not only on the battlefield in one's physical death, but continued after death as one's spirit faithfully served the nation. In addition, the rhetoric of fidelity and the call to arms through self-

---

[38] Holtom, D.C. *Modern Japan and Shinto Nationalism*. 1947; rpt. New York: Paragon Book Reprint Corporation, 1963, p. 47.

[39] The word "goshi" means to confer the status of a Shinto diety upon a deceased person.

sacrifice as indicated in the Rescript of 1868 became a template on which nationalism would be patterned up to the present day. Within the Shrine's precincts today, the ideology of self-sacrifice is exhibited through World War II memorabilia such as human guided torpedoes and a fighter pilot's bomber jacket pierced by several bullets.

In keeping with its special status, Yasukuni was funded and administered differently from other Shinto Shrines. The Emperor allotted the shrine enough farmland to generate an unusually large income of over 50,000 bushels of rice a year.[40] While the finances supporting other shrines fluctuated dramatically during the Meiji period, the government's sponsorship of Yasukuni never wavered.[41] Moreover, while the management of ordinary Shinto shrines shifted from one agency to another, Yasukuni was administered by the Ministry of War from its inception. Its construction was personally supervised by the War Ministry's Vice Minister,O mura Masujiro, and its ceremonies and rituals were conducted by military officers rather than trained Shinto priests.[42]

As Japan's economic capacity and military ambition expanded in the late

---

[40]   Candler, Clayton. "Meet Me at Yasukuni! Postwar Japanese Nationalism and the Shrine of the 'Tranquil land.'" Undergraduate Honors Thesis, Harvard University, 1985, p. 22.

[41]   Fane, Richard A. B. Ponsonby. The Vicissitudes of Shinto. Kakikamo, Kyoto: The Ponsonby Memorial Society, 1963, p. 122.

[42]   Fane, The Vicissitudes of Shinto, p. 122.

31

Meiji period, Yasukuni assumed even greater significance. The increasing tally of war dead enshrined at Yasukuni was indicative of the Shrine's ideological potency as an instrument of nationalism. Over 13,000 war dead were enshrined during the Sino-Japanese War in the 1890s and more than 86,000 dead were enshrined following the Russo-Japanese War (1904-1905).[43] After the Marco Polo Bridge incident in 1937, the Shrine began interring large numbers of soldiers on an annual basis: 14,866 in 1938; 20,768 in 1939; 27,199 in 1940; and 29,989 in 1941.[44]

By World War II, as these figures imply, the Imperial Army and Navy had manipulated Yasukuni into a national symbol of aggression and ultranationalism. The Shrine was expropriated as a religious institution sanctioning the government's political agenda and the military's imperialistic objectives. Yasukuni stood at the iconographic center of Japanese nationalism and symbolized the military's mission to secure a sense of international prestige, glorify Japan's modern imperial achievements, and unify the nation's hearts and minds. The Shrine also assumed the role of contributor to the psychological appeal of the Emperor's divinity: "All enshrinements were ordered by the emperor, the emperor visited it more frequently than any other shrine except for

[43]   Oe, "Yasukuni Jinja mondai," p. 16.

[44]   Woodard, "Yasukuni Shrine," p. 73.

the Grand Shrine at Ise, and imperial gifts to the Shrine were frequent and generous."[45] Moreover, the possibility of deification and veneration by the emperor himself was open to every soldier who gave his life in battle.[46]

The Meiji Emperor paid tribute at Yasukuni seven times, the Taisho Emperor twice, and prior to Japan's surrender in 1945, Emperor Hirohito visited the Shrine twenty times, always donned in military apparel and acting in the capacity of supreme commander of the Imperial forces.[47] Each visit was a continuous reminder of the Emperor's endorsement and legitimation of the country's goals. Each death in his name fortified the spiritual and psychological appeal of emperorism, ethnocentrism, aggression, and nationalism. During World War II Hirohito became the primary figurehead condoning the Ministry of War's policy of imperialism and aggression. His attendance at Yasukuni and his prayers for the fallen war dead invoked a powerful image in the Japanese mind. His ritual acts and condolences for the families were simultaneously an appeal for continuing sacrifice. The extent to which the emperor ideology had been successfully imbued within the mindset of the Japanese people - - and specifically military personnel - - was expressed by Japanese pilots during

---

[45]   Woodard, "Yasukuni Shrine," p. 77.

[46]   Woodard, "Yasukuni Shrine," p. 77.

[47]   Oe, "Yasukuni Jinja mondai," p. 91.

World War II. Before embarking on *kamikaze* bombing raids, it was said that they shouted to their comrades the words, "Meet me at Yasukuni!"[48]

At Yasukuni, religion and state became intimately connected through the repetition of time-honored Shinto rituals and the elaborate displays of military might. Japan's role in World War II was conceived and perceived as the nation's Imperial mission. Religion and state were one and the same.

---

[48]   Chandler, "Meet me At Yasukuni!'," p. 2.

Chapter II   Postwar Japan: A "New Vision"

This grand ideological scheme came crashing down with Japan's surrender in 1945. Yasukuni was officially dismantled ideologically on December 15 when American Occupation authorities issued the so-called "Shinto Directive." The order prohibited the state from participating in religious affairs and forbade the Shrine from receiving state funding. The separation of politics and religion was further ensured through Articles 20 and 89 of the 1947 Constitution which accorded all Japanese the freedom of religion and required the state and its organs to refrain from religious education or any religious activity:

> The Shinto Directive was designed to free the Japanese people from direct or indirect compulsion to believe or profess to believe in a religion or cult officially designated by the state, to lift from the Japanese people the burden of compulsory financial support of an ideology which had contributed to the war guilt, defeat, suffering, privation and current deplorable condition, to prevent a recurrence of the perversion of Shinto theory and beliefs into militaristic and ultranationalistic propaganda designed to delude the people and lead them into wars of aggression, and to assist them in a rededication of their national life to building a new Japan based upon the ideal of perpetual peace and democracy.[49]

But the Occupation authorities fell short of expunging nationalistic consciousness from the Japanese. Over the course of a century, Yasukuni had

---

[49]   Woodard, William P.   *The Allied Occupation of Japan 1945 - 1952 and*

become deeply rooted as the historical and spiritual center for honoring the nation's war dead.[50]

If the Shinto Directive was aimed, at least in part, toward removing all the religious symbols that promoted ultranationalism and hindered the growth of democratic sentiments, why did the Occupation authorities allow Yasukuni to remain? One reason is that despite its purely instrumental origins, by the war's end Yasukuni had assumed an undeniably religious significance for millions of Japanese. Therefore, it could not be destroyed without violating the principle of religious freedom as guaranteed by Article 20 of Japan's new Constitution.

Though space does not permit a detailed analysis of the SCAP (Supreme Commander of the Allied Powers) directives to quell ultranationalistic ideology, suffice it to say that the occupation reforms stopped short of eliminating State Shinto because they recognized that Shinto was not inherently dangerous, but had only been exploited by the Japanese government for nationalistic purposes.

Daniel Holtom raised a related argument in his Modern Japan and

---

Japanese Religions. Leiden: E. J. Brill, 1972., p. 68.

[50] In compliance with a state directive issued in 1939, every prefecture was to have one official "Defense-of-the-Nation Shrine." Whereas Yasukuni represented a sanctuary on the state level, "Defense-of-the-Nation Shrines" created an intricate network at the grassroots level by duplicating the apotheosis. At the most local level, there were stone markers called chu konshi. From Field, Norma. In the Realm of the Dying Emperor, New York, Pantheon Books, 1991, p. 120.

Shinto Nationalism (1946):

> It is no part of the proper operation of a conquering power to deny a defeated enemy the right to carry out ceremonies in honor of its war dead, even though the cause for which they died is believed to have been a mistaken one. It is not sufficient to leave these rights to a private religious sect. They have a national importance; they are affectionately regarded as part of the magnificent tradition, probably its most tender part, and to close them to national celebration is only to feed the flames of resentment and bitterness.[51]

The Occupation authorities' willingness to allow Yasukuni's continued existence seems to have stemmed from their understanding that as long as the Shrine remained a private religious organization removed from potential manipulation by the state, it posed no threat as a tool of militarism.[52] Moreover, as Holtom suggests, the Yasukuni Shrine was a cultural manifestation of nationalism that acquired an aura of sacredness. It was a physical representation of patriotic emotion and a symbol of national identity nourished over sixty years. To desecrate this symbol would have been an "insult to the state if not an outright crime," and an insult to the imperial family, which SCAP hoped to use.[53]

SCAP authorities intended to preserve the office of the emperor to maintain stability in Japan while their democratic policies were being

---

[51] Holtom, *Modern Japan and Shinto Nationalism*, p. 206.

[52] Creemers, Wilhelmus H. M. *Shrine Shinto after World War II*. Leiden, Netherlands: E.J. Brill, 1968, p. 162.

[53] Goodman and Refsing, *Ideology and Practice in Modern Japan*, p. 27.

implemented. SCAP officials "transformed the emperor from sovereign to symbol, but retained both the office and the person, Hirohito . . . . [They believed] the emperor provided a continuity useful to postwar reform."[54] The emperor was no longer viewed by many as a rallying point for the revival of Japanese ultranationalism but rather a useful tool for encouraging democracy in Japan and promoting unity during a crucial time. Furthermore, he was viewed by occupation officials at the time as a "bulwark" against Russian Communism.[55]

*   *   *

With the end of the American occupation of Japan on April 28, 1952, Japanese began to discuss the re-nationalization of the Yasukuni Shrine in public. During the fifties, members of the Nihon Izokukai began to mobilize and initiated a movement to press for the restoration of official patronage for Yasukuni. In 1960, the Nihon Izokukai submitted a formal request to the Diet and the government for the restoration of state subsidization and administration

---

[54]   Carol Gluck, "The Past in the Present," 64-95.

[55]   Robert E. Ward and Frank Joseph Shulman. The Allied Occupation of Japan, 1945-1952: An Annotated Bibliography of Western Language Materials. Chicago: The American Library Association, 1974., pp. 57, 414 and 416. Also, "Hirohito: Criminal or Puppet?" U.S. News & World Report., 17 March 1950, 20-21.

of the Yasukuni Shrine.[56] Many members of the Nihon Izokukai "recognized the Yasukuni Shrine as the central institution for mourning the war dead."[57] By the mid-sixties, debate over the resurrection of Yasukuni to its prewar status had permeated the Diet. From 1964 through 1974, the Liberal Democratic Party (LDP) annually submitted the Yasukuni Shrine Bill to the Diet calling for the nationalization of the Shrine. In most cases, the bill was withdrawn due to strong protest from opposition parties.[58]

The Liberal Democratic Party was established in November 1955 through the merger of two prewar conservative parties, the Japan Liberal Party and the Japan Progressive Party. The LDP's conservative platform was based on "traditional and civic values such as patriotism, deference to authority, respect for the institution of the family, and belief in law and order."[59] However, the LDP's ideological camp is by no means monolithic and party lines on national policy have often been divided by contradictory positions. Among the more

---

[56]   Creemers, "Shrine Shinto after World War II," pp. 169-170.

[57]   Hayashi Shuzo. "Kakuryo no Yasukuni Jinja sanpai mondai kodankai no ho kokusho ni tsuite" (Regarding the Report of the Roundtable on the issue of Official Visits to Yasukuni Shrine by Cabinet Members). Jurisuto, vol. 848, 1985: 40.

[58]   Chandler, "Meet Me at Yasukuni," p. 5.

[59]   Kodansha Encyclopedia of Japan. (Tokyo: Kodansha Ltd., 1993), s.v. "Liberal Democratic Party," by Haruhiro Fukui.

renowned examples of internal party dissent are the LDP's promotion of academic freedom and liberal education while simultaneously supporting government control of school textbooks and teachers. Defense issues have been contentious and the LDP has called for an independent self-defense force within the "framework of mutual defense arrangements with the United States."[60] There has also been a diversity of opinions among LDP members regarding the revision of Japan's Constitution.

As a legislative approach to reinstating Yasukuni did not seem promising, the LDP sought a new means to its ends. In 1975, Prime Minister Miki Takeo became the first postwar Prime Minister to make a formal visit to Yasukuni Shrine. To substantiate that his visit to the Shrine was as a *private citizen* rather than in his official capacity as Prime Minister, Miki used a private car to travel to Yasukuni, did not sign his title in the shrine registry, and contributed to the Shrine from his own pocket.[61]

Over the next nine years, each of Prime Minister Miki's successors made an "unofficial" visit to Yasukuni and each one grew a little more flexible in their definition of "unofficial." In 1978, Fukuda Takeo used his official title in the

---

[60]   *Kodansha Encyclopedia of Japan*. *(Tokyo: Kodansha Ltd., 1993), s.v. "Liberal Democratic Party," by Haruhiro Fukui.*

[61]   *"Prime Minister's Visit to Yasukuni," The Japan Times Weekly, International Edition, August 26, 1978, p. 12.*

registry.[62] In 1979, within a few months of the enshrinement of 14 Class-A war criminals,O hira Masayoshi visited the Shrine despite the fact that he was a Christian.[63] In 1982, Suzuki Zenko worshipped at Yasukuni along with his entire cabinet and 200 LDP Dietmen. He also refused to reveal whether he worshipped in his public or his private capacity.[64]

It was not until 1985 that Nakasone Yasuhiro became the first postwar Prime Minister to declare his visit to the Shrine as official. Rather than follow the established procedure for formal worship at a shrine, which encompasses the offering of a sprig of the sacred *sakaki* tree, bowing twice, clapping twice, and bowing once more, Nakasone offered flowers purchased with government funds and bowed only once. This display, as Norma Field concludes, was designed to dodge objections based on the separation of religion and state as well as cloak the ritual in non-religious garb.[65] In response to the severe domestic and international criticism he attracted, Nakasone urged the government to form a

---

[62] *"Prime Minister's Visit to Yasukuni," August 26, 1978, p. 12.*

[63] *"The Yasukuni Issue: Christian Prime Minister's Visit to Shrine Stirs Controversy," The Japan Times Weekly, International Edition, May 5, 1979.*

[64] *"Suzuki, Ministers Defy Critics, Pay Homage at Yasukuni Shrine," The Japan Times Weekly, International Edition, August 16, 1982, p. 2.*

[65] *Field, In the Realm of a Dying Emperor, p. 140. The sakaki is a species of evergreen, with shinny-topped leaves that attract deities to alight on them. During the enshrinement ceremony the branch becomes the deity incarnate.*

commission to address the Yasukuni problem. Subsequently, this too inspired a barrage of criticism from various opponents.

According to a New York Times article reporting on Nakasone's visit to Yasukuni, China's Foreign Ministry was quoted as having said that the visit would have "a harmful effect on the feelings of Chinese and other Asians occupied by Japan in the 1930s and 1940s."[66] The Beijing Review called Nakasone's visit "a jarring note amid the universal calls for peace and justice," and hoped that the Japanese government would "bow to the historical facts and take an unequivocal stand on where the guilt and the responsibility for its appalling war of aggression" lay.[67]

Within Japan, opposition parties vigorously attacked Nakasone, insinuating that his official display was intended to garner support for LDP policies. The Socialist Party said that the visit was "intended to coincide with a

---

[66] Clyde Haberman, "Tokyo 40 Years Later: War Dead are Honored," The New York Times, 16 August 1985, p. 2.

[67] Xin Jong, "Nakasone's Shrine Visit Draws Fire," Beijing Review 28 (September 1985): 12. Nakasone's visit touched off bitter criticisms in China, Korea, Taiwan, and Southeast Asia not only because of Japanese atrocities committed on their soil, but because Shinto was impressed upon the citizens of those countries while under Japanese occupation. Shinto shrines were often erected in those colonies. In Taipei, the Japanese built the Taiwan Shrine, in Seoul the Chosen Shrine, and the Shonan Shrine in Singapore. Fukatsu Masumi, "A State Visit to Yasukuni Shrine," Japan Quarterly, Vol. 33, No. 1, (January-April, 1986).

bigger military build-up."[68] In response to Nakasone's call for a task force to study the Yasukuni issue, the Socialist Party stated, "No reports prepared by the advisory councils can alter the government's unified opinion declared in the process of Diet debate. Official worship at the Shrine means the negation of the government's duty to observe the Constitution."[69] An editorial in the Japan Times suggested that the debate over Yasukuni and use of "private advisory groups" revealed an interesting facet of Nakasone's politics. According to the editorial:

> Mr. Nakasone's clever use of inner groups of trusted private persons have been helping to sugar-coat his rather hawkish stance with an outward semblance of democratic procedure in producing solutions to sensitive problems.[70]

Why has the LDP, and specifically those Prime Ministers who held office between 1975 and 1985, embraced the Yasukuni Shrine so vigorously? Why has it considered the Shrine important and pressed the issue with so much so zeal? One reason why the LDP embraced the Yasukuni cause was because the Shrine provided it with a strong symbol around which it could gather support for

---

[68] *Hikaru Kerns, "Fury Over Nakasone Tribute to War Dead," The London Times, 16 August 1985, p. 5.*

[69] *"Official Yasukuni Visits May Be Allowable: Advisory Panel," The Japan Times International Edition, 10 August 1985, p. 4.*

[70] *"An Aspect of Nakasone's Politics," The Japan Times, 23 August 1985, p. 44.*

its conservative policies. The LDP sought to remain politically active and competitive by attracting powerful support groups who believed Yasukuni and other national symbols were necessary to the survival of Japanese identity. The LDP became the public voice - - and, to some extent, the puppet - - of the Nihon Izokukai, who used the LDP to promote their desire for the nationalization of Yasukuni as a memorial to the war dead.

In surveying relevant news articles, it appears that the LDP gained the political backing of the Nihon Izokukai (while simultaneously pacifying them as a potentially adversarial group), by taking up the Shrine issue. On August 16, 1992, the Japan Times printed the wish of one war-bereaved member who expressed her hopes that "Cabinet members visit [Yasukuni] because the war dead devoted their lives to the fatherland, complying with the government's requests."[71] In this sense, LDP support was viewed as the government's official act of reciprocation and appreciation for the sacrifices of so many war dead. In any case, the Nihon Izokukai had a history of publically squeezing the LDP politically when it did not honor the group's wishes. In 1986, after Nakasone announced his plan to cancel his trip to Yasukuni due to international criticism, the Nihon Izokukai withdrew 160,000 of its members from the LDP in protest.

---

[71]   "Worshippers Favor Visits by Officials," The Japan Times, 16 August 1992.

44

However, regardless of such heavy-handed political tactics and strategies, the Yasukuni Shrine issue had a slightly different purpose for Prime Minister Nakasone.[72]

*   *   *

The formal request to settle the Yasukuni issue came on the order of Prime Minister Nakasone Yasuhiro whose conservative political agenda included the dispelling of certain sensitive issues which hindered Japan's domestic activities and emerging international character. Long known as an advocate of constitutional revision, Japanese rearmament and the termination of Japan's Security Treaty, Nakasone arrived in office in 1982 "declaring that it was time to address hitherto taboo topics and 'settle all accounts' on postwar political issues."[73] His adamant devotion to this mission was apparent even early on in his career as a politician.

Having returned home in the autumn of 1945 after fighting in the war as an Imperial Japanese Navy Officer, Nakasone bore witness to the psychological and material devastation that the war had wrought upon Japan. In his autobiographical memoir, Nakasone Yasuhiro: My Life in Politics, Nakasone

---

[72]   "Nakasone Calls off Shrine Trip," The Japan Times, 15 August 1986, p. 7.

[73]   Pyle, Kenneth B. The Japanese Question: Power and Purpose in a New Era. Washington, D.C.: The AEI Press, 1992, p. 85.

45

wrote:

> I felt humiliated that Japan had been defeated and forced into unconditional surrender. The many accomplishments achieved over the two-thirds of a century of modernization and industrialization following the opening of Japan in the Meiji Restoration had been reduced to dust. We had lost control of our destiny; we were subjected to the authority of the Supreme Commander of Allied Powers (SCAP). I could not stand by idly without criticizing those former leaders who had brought on a mistaken war, who had forced on the people a bitter struggle unmatched since the dawn of their nation, and who had left an ignoble blot on the annals of Japanese history. But criticizing former leaders was not enough. I wanted to help rebuild my homeland. I felt keenly my responsibility toward history. I wanted to do everything possible to restore Japan's strength, to hasten the return of independence and stability to the Japanese people.[74]

Although he envisaged a "newly reborn Japan," Nakasone also accepted the fact that the nation could not rebuild along the same path of "parochial, self-centered nationalism" it had followed before the war.[75] Keenly aware of the conditions in the immediate postwar era, Nakasone decided to run for a seat in the House of Representatives, specifically the Liberal Democratic Party, emerging victorious in April 1947 and becoming the youngest member of the Diet at 28 years old.

As a member of the Diet, Nakasone was confronted with paradoxical circumstances and challenged by a very bureaucratized political system. He

---

[74] Sayer, Nat. _Nakasone, Yasuhiro: My Life in Politics._ (draft of translation), p. 5-6. Nat Sayer was one of Nakasone's trusted American "brains"

[75] Nakasone, _My Life in Politics_, p. 8.

was caught in the vacuum between the collapse of Japan's prewar state and the ensuing postwar settlement. He was faced with the opportunity to become an architect and potential leader of a new postwar order in Japan, and he strongly felt the necessity of establishing some sense of national heritage, pride and purpose for the spiritually impoverished Japanese people. Although he acknowledged the need for Japan to rebuild according to "universal principles which could be understood and shared" throughout the entire world, he also believed in the necessity for Japan to develop a sense of nationalism in order to remain unified and to survive as a nation during both the American Occupation and the inevitable internationalization of Japan.[76]

*   *   *

Among Nakasone's more pressing agenda issues was his dedication to securing a more autonomous defense force for Japan. With that focus, he sought to overturn the San Francisco Peace Treaty of September 8, 1951. This highly unequal treaty between Japan and the United States granted the U.S. the right to maintain military bases in Japan, the right to employ military power from those bases without seeking prior permission from Japan, the right to veto any third country's military presence in Japan, and an indefinite time period for the

---

[76]   Nakasone, _My Life in Politics_, p. 8.

47

treaty.[77]

As an advocate of political nationalism, rather than economic nationalism, Nakasone believed Japan had surpassed the "catch-up" era long associated with his predecessors. Operating under an American military umbrella since the 1960s, Japan was accorded the luxury of devoting most of the nation's capital to economic and industrial reconstruction. Nakasone wanted Japan to use its newly created postwar economic wealth and power as the foundation of a new place for Japan in the world. For this reason, he was often branded a rabid neo-nationalist. Nevertheless, Nakasone asked the Japanese to rise up and fulfill their international responsibilities and help transform the nation into a global leader.

According to Pyle, there were four main tenets to Nakasone's "grand design" for Japan. The first was intended to demonstrate that Japan was no longer a follower nation. Nakasone envisioned Japan embracing a new and sophisticated "information society" founded upon a "new stage of human and technological development."[78] Symbolic of this phase was the creation of new telecommunication networks that balanced highly sophisticated Japanese technology with new groups of specialists and new societal behavior patterns.

---

[77]   Pyle, _Japanese Question_, p. 27.

[78]   Pyle, _Japanese Question_, p. 90.

Secondly, Nakasone insisted that Japan should be prepared for global leadership by being remodeled into an international state. This entailed reforming Japan's institutions to meet the foreign expectations of an internationalized Japan. In essence, Nakasone argued that Japan's institutions were primarily designed for rapid economic growth to catch-up with Western technology and industrialization. As an international state, Nakasone believed Japan would be expected to make her institutions more liberal and open to foreign economic affairs as a member of a competitive world market.[79]

Thirdly, Nakasone promoted a new form of nationalism that befitted his vision of Japan as an international state and global leader. He appreciated the fact that defeat and occupation by the United States stripped Japan's postwar generations of their sense of pride and national heritage. Therefore, he pressed the urgency for a "new" nationalism unimpeded by the old mentality of traditional nationalism. He encouraged international education to stimulate greater understanding and cooperation between Japan and the West, and he called for an appreciation of traditional Japanese institutions and history to reignite a sense of self-esteem and understanding of what it meant to be Japanese.[80]

Lastly, Nakasone called on Japan to assume an active role in global

---

[79]   Pyle, *Japanese Question*, pp. 90-93.

[80]   Pyle, *Japanese Question*, pp. 94-100.

49

strategic affairs. He was a staunch supporter of Japan's international right to defend herself and continued to state the importance of revising the Constitution to build a "strong Japan" for the twenty-first century.[81] In assessing these four convictions, one can easily understand why Nakasone was often portrayed simultaneously as an articulate international statesman dedicated to the promulgation of peace, and also a loyal supporter of traditional Japanese values. These were the two contradictory images with which he would have to contend with when addressing sensitive postwar issues.

Nakasone's political rhetoric and romantic vision found expression in his handling of the controversial Yasukuni Shrine issue. He advocated his "new vision" of Japan as an international leader by attaching importance to this traditional institution and its history, believing its significance as a symbol could foster a strong sense of self-confidence and national pride. To Nakasone,

> The [Yasukuni] issue offered a symbolic way of putting the war aside as a source of national shame and embarrassment and returning to traditional reverence for the spirits of the war dead . . . it showed the gratitude of the people for the sacrifices made by their forbears.[82]

In the larger political context, Nakasone used Yasukuni as a political tool to fuel his vision of Japan. As mentioned above, he believed the nation had the

---

[81]   Pyle, *Japanese Question*, p. 102.

[82]   Pyle, *Japanese Question*, p. 99.

potential to propel ahead technologically and economically, and to assume the role of international leader. In turn, a "new" nationalism would be founded, one which was characterized by Japan's international pursuits. Historians writing on the subject of Japanese nationalism and Nakasone's politics found themselves rather perplexed over the use of a traditional symbol in a self-consciously advanced and highly technological age. According to Pyle, Japan no longer needed to rely on "traditional symbols" for a sense of pride and patriotism. Japanese nationalism "builds on Japan's industrial accomplishments and finds confidence from achieving Western ends by Japanese means."[83] In other words, it was felt that the Japanese were riding on their remarkable political, social and institutional transformations since the end of World War II and there was no longer any reason to rely on the past to build the future. The future was being created in the present which was uninformed by the past.

However, what politicians and scholars had labeled a "new nationalism" or "internationalism" was nothing more than what the Christian Activity News called, "a kimono of another color."[84] The external appearance may have

---

[83]   Pyle, *The Japanese Question*, p. 97. Also, "Our Internationalization or Yours?," *The Japan Times*, 22 September 1988 and "A New Japanese Nationalism," *The New York Times*, 12 April 1987.

[84]   "Yasukuni In New Dress." *Japan Christian Activity News*, 10 February 1972, p. 4.

changed, but the underlying fabric and texture remained unaltered. Recreating nationalism under the alias of international activities did not divert the original nationalistic message and mission which remained indisputably linked to the past. Japanese nationalism was merely re-clothed by contemporary analysts. Ensconced under the guise of a new character and name, postwar Japanese nationalism was (and remains) a modern method of shoring-up domestic pride in the country in order to achieve postwar *Japanese ends through Japanese means*, while constructing the outward affectations of an internationalist world power. It is also the contention of this author that postwar Japanese national historiography has been written with the naive belief, specifically among Western scholars, that the American occupation of Japan cleanly severed the past from the present, leaving no strains of nationalistic continuity visible in the postwar era.

Under Nakasone's leadership, the rhetoric of internationalism was employed to rebuild a sense of national unity that was fragmented by the occupation authorities. However, what scholars and politicians have construed as internationalism has actually been a continuation of Japan's historical quest for respect, a longing for recognition as a member of the international community, and a tool to enhance the glorification of Japan's achievements.

The Yasukuni Shrine provided a useful symbolic foundation upon which

52

Nakasone could build his international political platform while sustaining some measure of cultural continuity, or so he believed. The advisory group he established to reach a consensus on the issue consisted of members hand-picked by Nakasone himself. His political stratagem entailed the frequent use of commissions to study and suggest recommendations on contentious issues of national importance. According to Kenji Hayao's The Japanese Prime Minister and Public Policy,

> One of the problems with the prime minister's institutional support is that it furnishes virtually no policy advice or expertise apart from what the bureaucracy provides. There have been a number of attempts to give the prime minister policy aides, but they have all failed because of opposition from the bureaucracy and many members of the LDP. The bureaucracy has been adamantly opposed; it prefers that the prime minister not have the organization to make decisions by himself so that it can continue to draw up the drafts for policy. LDP members are afraid that a system of prime ministerial aides would allow the prime minister to act independently of the party.[85]

To circumvent these political obstacles, Nakasone developed his "New Vision" proposals independently, and strategically exerted his control over policy making by using "advisory committees staffed for the most part by his personal advisers, his 'brain.'" For example, Nakasone appropriated 20 million yen toward the construction of a new Japanese Studies institute which was to begin work on re-

---

[85] *Hayao Kenji. The Japanese Prime Minister and Public Policy. Pittsburgh: University of Pittsburgh Press, 1993, p. 180.*

establishing Japanese identity. In charge of the institute was Umehara Takeshi, who was also one of the members chosen by Nakasone to be on the commission to study and settle the Yasukuni Shrine problem.[86]

Nakasone used these committees aggressively to establish a "top-down presidential-style prime ministership," and appointed to them those who were personally and philosophically close to him and the issues he believed in:

> This method of establishing public and private advisory bodies outside the party, filling them with people one liked, appealing to public opinion with their reports, and thereby guiding policy, was suited to Nakasone's personal preference. It also suggested that . . . the Nakasone faction lacked troop strength and consequently was unable to adopt the traditional LDP approach of bureaucratic policy formulation and intraparty maneuvering.[87]

Nakasone's radical and unorthodox methods were a direct result of his frustration with the decision-making process ingrained within the Japanese political system. In Europe and the United States, decisions are made at the top,

---

[86]   Buruma, Ian. "A New Japanese Nationalism," _The New York Times Magazine_. 12 April 1987, 23-38. As one of Japan's foremost "Yamatoists," Umehara Takeshi has stated that Western civilization is a disease threatening the world and he believes the only cure can be found within the pristine state of the Japanese soul, which can be traced back 12,000 years to the Jomon period. Yamatoists like Umehara and conservative literary critics such as Eto Jun have also lambasted the American occupation for "destroying the continuity of Japanese culture." It is their opinion that the Japanese must preserve their traditions and keep sacred the Japanese soul in order to ward off the harmful effects of Westernization.

[87]   Masumi Junnosuke. _Contemporary Politics in Japan_. Berkeley: University of California Press, p. 422.

but in Japan, which has been referred to as a "consensus society," decisions often percolate from the bottom up. Essentially, Japanese political culture is characterized by decisions which are made only after "sufficient time has passed for the conflicting interests and opinions to be brought into accord and a consensus formed."[88] This socially oriented construct has ensured the perpetuation of such prized values as group harmony and political and economic stability and continuity.[89]

Irrespective of his critics, Nakasone pursued his personal style of political creativity. Looking back over his thirty-seven year career since the end of World War II, Nakasone wrote that the world had experienced vast changes in politics, the economy and society. "Rapid change," he said, "always gives rise to new problems, and there likewise is always a need for innovative approaches to overcoming the new challenges that go beyond conventional thinking and political styles."[90]

The Yasukuni Shrine became an integral political cornerstone during Nakasone's administration because it represented a microcosm of his idealistic international vision. Nakasone believed he could sway government policy on

---

[88] Nakasone, *My Life in Politics*, p. 2.

[89] Nakasone, *My Life in Politics*, p. 2.

[90] Nakasone, *My Life in Politics*, p. 1.

Yasukuni by channelling the debate outside of mainstream politics and through a special advisory commission. But, in the end, Nakasone's end-run strategy would lead only to frustration.

Chapter III   The Inquiry

On August 3, 1984, Chief Cabinet Secretary Fujinami Takao convened a fifteen member advisory Commission chaired by Hayashi Keizo to study the Yasukuni problem.[91] The Hayashi Commission was organized to investigate various predicaments associated with the legal, religious and social problems involved in official visits to the Shrine by the Prime Minister and Cabinet members.[92] The Commission was comprised mainly of persons outside of government, including academicians, authors, businessmen, jurists, and former high-ranking bureaucrats, thus representing - - in theory - - a cross-section of society (see Appendix A for a listing of the panel members and short biographical sketches). Although these members deliberated on twenty-one occasions during the allotted year, they were unable to reach a consensus on the issue, produce a unified report, or offer the Cabinet Secretary a recommendation. In their written report submitted on August 9, 1985, the Commission unanimously decided to represent all of the opinions expounded on

---

[91]   "Kokuryo no Yasukuni Jinja sanpai de kondankai" (Roundtable Discussion on Official Visits to the Yasukuni Shrine by Cabinet Members). *Asahi Nenkan*, 1985, p. 84.

[92]   "Yasukuni Shrine Debate Begins," *The Japan Times Weekly*. August 18, 1984, p. 3.

the issue.[93]

The four page report was published on November 10, 1985 in a journal entitled Jurisuto (Jurist). This journal covers public interest issues of a legal and economic nature and caters to a well-informed popular readership. The specific issue used in this study is devoted entirely to the Yasukuni problem and lists the names of all fifteen Commission members, although their opinions are cited anonymously. The journal also includes eighteen commentaries on related issues debated by the Commission, providing additional insights and a more thorough investigation of the ideas represented in the official written report.

No Western scholars have thoroughly explained the multitude of impasses the Commission members confronted when considering the political, religious and social aspects of the Yasukuni problem. According to Hardacre, the writers of the report were split in three ways: those favoring official visits to the Shrine by the Prime Minister and Cabinet members, those opposed to it, and a faction advocating the construction of an entirely new national monument for the war dead, "one that would be free of the religious and political implications bound up with the Yasukuni Shrine."[94] The first two categorizations will be

---

[93]   "Kakuryo no Yasukuni Jinja sanpai mondai ni kan suru kondankai ho kokusho" (Report of the roundtable on the issue of Official Visits to Yasukuni Shrine by Cabinet Members). Jurisuto, vol. 848, 1985, p. 110.

[94]   Hardacre, Shinto amd the State, p. 150.

adopted in essence, but in this study will be referred to as the conservatives and the progressives, respectively. These titles follow Pyle's investigation of the Japanese intellectual milieu from the 1960s through the 1980s.[95] The third group, representing only a small constituency as can best be deciphered from the report, will be referred to as the "compromise faction."

Before examining the written report, it will prove helpful to briefly outline the postwar political platforms of the conservatives and progressives in order to understand the origins and nature of their contending schools of thought. The opinions stated in the official report mainly reflect these two general categories.

Carol Gluck has taken a particularly stimulating approach in categorizing and characterizing these two "custodians of the past." She suggests that both the conservatives and progressives have written and re-written history according to their postwar experiences, producing "different histories that vied with one another for legitimation and dominance."[96] Both groups have competed

---

[95] For more information on the schools of thought that emerged amidst the changing conditions and attitudes of postwar Japan, see Kenneth Pyle. "The Future of Japanese Nationality: An Essay in Contemporary History." Journal of Japanese Studies, vol.8, no. 2 (1982): 223-263. This essay examines four contending schools of thought that conducted their political debates in general interest magazines such as Chuo Koron, Bungei Shunju, Voice, and Shokun. Also, Koschmann, Victor J. "Intellectuals and Politics." in Postwar Japan as History, ed. Andrew Gordon, 395-423. Berkeley, University of California Press, 1993.

[96] Gluck, "Past in the Present," p. 65.

vigorously to instill within public memory their brand of postwar history in order to shape the course of Japan's future. They have relied on the past to influence their political stance in the present. While conservatives view prewar Japanese history as the foundation of postwar Japan, the progressives repeatedly articulate the period prior to 1945 as "past history" and refer to the end of World War II as a "sharp rupture" in Japanese history.

While there are different degrees of conservatism in contemporary Japan, many conservative thinkers seem to advocate similar policies and national concerns. Above all, they seek continuity with the past and the maintenance of the status quo. The conservative faction of the LDP has tended to support the revision of Japan's Constitution as well as the Security Treaty with the United States. Conservatives maintain the right to rearmament and, in general, believe Japan should "pursue a more autonomous and independent course (Although one not detrimental to Japan's traditional moral foundations and national character)."[97] Many of these neo-nationalists concur with textbook revisions and the clouding of Japan's aggressive role in World War II:

> For them, the war revealed no fundamental flaw of national character, nor even fault on the prewar emperor system. It was rather [perceived as] an aberration -- an interlude in which military conspiracy, left-wing planning, and diplomatic blunders deflected the Japanese from their legitimate goals pursued since the Meiji

---

[97] *Pyle, The Japanese Question, p. 31.*

60

Restoration.[98]

In the past, mainstream conservatives have also supported the revival of Japan's role as leader in Asia.

The progressives, on the other hand, emerged from the postwar reform period offering the country a more forward looking platform upon which to rebuild national character in the face of defeat and destruction. They supported the new democratic order constructed for Japan by the United States and promoted the guarantees inscribed in the new Constitution. In the 1960s, their ideas developed out of "wartime disillusion," the rejection of prewar Japanese nationalism, and a "profound distrust" of traditional administrative policies. The progressives believed the Japanese people had been "victimized by a reactionary leadership that indoctrinated them in an artificial nationalism," and had therefore "shown the demented course of the modern nation-state by its aggressions in Asia."[99]

As critics of the status quo, the progressives' vision of Japan was that of a peaceful nation, one that had rejected the use of arms, recognized the ills of

---

[98]   Pyle, *The Japanese Question*, p. 17.

[99]   Pyle, *The Japanese Question*, p. 45.

prewar state power, and was now determined to move forward as a modern industrial nation capable of leading the world toward a peaceful international order.[100] The discourse of this "utopian mission" and progressive attempts to transform national character invited a barrage of attacks from conservatives in the 1970s. As the progressives espoused the democratic ideals in the Constitution and forswore the intrusion of imperial ideology, conservatives accused them of abandoning their own nation's history and traditions. In the 1980s, however, the appeal of progressive thought diminished as Japan excelled economically and began to exhibit a new self-confidence.

The intellectual and political debates between the conservatives and progressives continued with fervor over the Yasukuni Shrine issue. With the LDP in power and Nakasone's intention to remake national character through traditional institutions, Yasukuni sparked a period of intellectual ferment and became an exciting arena where cultural, social and intellectual issues clashed. The written report produced by the Hayashi Commission illustrates that the Yasukuni problem was, and still remains, an issue deadlocked in debate in the midst of Japan's pluralistic postwar political culture.

        *   *   *

One of the central issues among the Commission's discussions was the

---

[100]   Pyle, _The Japanese Question_, p. 45.

constitutionality of official visits to Yasukuni by government employees. On this matter, the Commission unanimously agreed to re-evaluate the shrine issue by employing legal precedent. However, the constitutionality of formal visits had never been challenged in the past and therefore, there were no previous examples to assist in guiding the Commission's inquiry.[101]

Prior to 1985, litigation promoting the official patronage of Yasukuni was either withdrawn or not taken seriously as Prime Ministers never declared whether their visits were actually conducted in their formal capacities. There was, therefore, no judicial reason to re-assess the law. In the past, visits to the Shrine by government leaders may have agitated some opposition groups, but as long as the nature of their visit remained ambiguous, they remained within the confines of the law. However, Nakasone's official visit presented a new situation. As a means of addressing the controversy in its present state, and in their search for some legal basis to work from, the Commission adopted the Supreme Court's decision on the Ground Breaking Ceremony in the city of Tsu (*Tsujichinsai*), as their model.[102] This judgement was handed down on July 13, 1977.

When the city of Tsu erected a municipal gymnasium in 1965, a

---

[101]   *Jurisuto*, "Kakuryo no Yasukuni Jinja sanpai mondai," p. 110.

[102]   *Jurisuto*, p. 111. The city of Tsu is located in central Japan's Mie Prefecture.

traditional Shinto ceremony was held for the laying of the cornerstone. The city was brought to court and accused of having violated Article 20 of the Constitution. The court ruled that the Shinto ceremony was a "social custom" rather than a "religious rite," and therefore it did not violate the law of separation between religion and state.[103] Furthermore, the court declared that among activities of the state and its organs, "any activity whose purpose has a religious significance, or whose effect leads to support, assistance, promotion, oppression of, or interference in, religion" is prohibited by Article 20, Section 3 of the Constitution.[104]

According to the Commission, the Supreme Court's judgement did not entirely negate Cabinet visits to the Shrine. The Court defended the principles underlining the separation of religion and state as written in the Constitution, but they did not define or clarify what constituted *religious activity* on the part of the government. Were official visits to Yasukuni considered to be a "social custom" or a "religious rite"? With this in mind and with a rather obscure model to work from, the commission decided to evaluate official visits to the Shrine by "giving careful consideration to the cultural and societal effects of official visits to Yasukuni Shrine in order to see whether they exceed the limitations of what is

---

[103]   Sakai, Takeshi. "A Matter of Faith," *Japan Quarterly*. 35, no. 4 (1988): pp. 357-364.

properly and legally allowed by law."[105]

The central issues of the debate addressed whether or not official visits were an expression of the government's will to intervene in private religious activity and, if so, whether or not these actions infringed upon the legal rights guaranteed to all citizens by the Constitution, specifically the freedom of religion. The Commission also considered whether State Shinto was being promoted and supported to the detriment of other religions, and whether these visits were a means of answering society's call for respect to the war dead on the part of the government.[106] The plethora of issues which arose from the Commission's brainstorming formed a complex web of problems intricately tied to the Shrine's history: interpretations of religion and religious activity, surreptitious government motives to remilitarize Japan, Japanese cultural history, American-imposed constitutional laws, and international politics and pressures.

The progressives seated on the Commission adamantly launched their protest against rehabilitating Yasukuni. According to their opinions in the report, reinstating the Yasukuni Shrine as a state-sanctioned religious institution was illegal. They asserted that any visits made by public officials represented a clear

---

[104]   *Jurisuto, p. 111.*

[105]   *Jurisuto, p. 111.*

[106]   *Jurisuto, p. 111.*

violation of Articles 20 and 89 of Japan's Constitution which supported the principle of separation between religion and the state.[107] They believed the government should be careful not to systematize formal visits because it could infringe on the rights of government officials as well as those of other citizens.[108] Conceivably, if paying a visit to Yasukuni was mandatory for all Cabinet members, then the right to freedom of religion would be violated.

According to the Commission, the legality of official visits hinged, in part, on whether Yasukuni was considered a religious institution still attached to its prewar holy character, or only a national memorial for the war dead.[109] If the Shrine was a national memorial, progressives questioned how it was possible for Cabinet members to use Shinto rituals without violating the Constitution. If they could not use traditional forms of worship, progressives wondered what forms would be appropriate.[110] The answers to these questions were left unresolved because the Commission members could not decide what would be constitutional and what would conform to the Supreme Court's 1977 decision.

Several progressive opinions stated that the Yasukuni Shrine was a

---

[107]   *Jurisuto*, p. 111.

[108]   *Jurisuto*, p. 113.

[109]   Hashimoto Kiminobu. *"Seikyo bunri to Yasukuni hokokusho" (Report of Yasukuni and the Separation of State and Religion)*. *Jurisuto*, vol. 848, 1985: p. 48.

religious enterprise by law and this made all visits illegal.[111]   Others, while understanding the *purpose* of these visits as secular, found the *effect* to produce an "intense symbolic meaning between state and religion that was reminiscent of the state's prewar employment of Shinto as a spiritual prop supporting aggression."[112] In general, the progressives were concerned with the revival of State Shinto, the suppression of other religions, and a resurgence of militarism. Official visits were therefore deemed unconstitutional in their opinion.

The conservatives' interpretation of official visits to the Shrine opposed both the Supreme Court's 1977 decision and the progressive's platform. The conservatives could not deny that these visits represented relations between the state and religion, but they did not believe these relations exceeded the law. Official visits were only an expression of the nation's conscience, they argued, and it had become customary in Japan for public dignitaries to pay a courtesy call to the Shrine.[113] In this light, official visits were interpreted as a "social custom" by some conservatives.   The conservatives believed official Cabinet visits represented an expression of human nature universally felt among the

---

[110]   *Jurisuto*, p. 111.

[111]   *Jurisuto*, p. 112.

[112]   *Jurisuto*, p. 112.

[113]   *Jurisuto*, p. 112.

peoples of all nations who have the right to mourn for their war dead. This feeling exceeded the boundaries of the state, the nation, and religion. Prayers for world peace and for the country were an integral part of mourning those who sacrificed their lives for the protection of their countrymen, children, parents, and country.[114] Thus they maintained that it was "natural" and "proper" for a Prime Minister to make official visits to the Shrine.[115]

To support their arguments, the conservatives raised an example which sparked further dissent among the Commission members. They noted that in many foreign countries, political leaders visit privately-run organizations as part of their public responsibilities. Such visits, whether deemed private or official, are considered public events in most cases because the leaders are constantly in the public's eye and are officials of the nation.[116] For this reason, conservatives felt that questions pertaining to the formality and informality of visits to Yasukuni were irrelevant.[117]

---

[114]   *Jurisuto*, p. 111.

[115]   *Hayashi Shuzo. "Kakuryo no Yasukuni Jinja sanpai mondai kodankai no ho kokusho ni tsuite" (Regarding the Report of the Roundtable on the issue of Official Visits to Yasukuni Shrine by Cabinet Members). Jurisuto, vol. 848, 1985: 40*

[116]   *Jurisuto*, p. 111.

[117]   *Although the written report does not compare Yasukuni Shrine to other national and international memorials, it should be noted that conservatives,*

In their rebuttal, the progressives argued that Prime Ministers and Cabinet members were public officials by vocation and all visits to the Shrine must therefore be considered official. In other words, the Yasukuni issue was not contingent upon the method of worship or whether public officials should be allowed into the Shrine's precincts to perform observances. Driving to the Shrine in an unofficial car, signing the registry without their title, and making an offering from their own paycheck had no bearing on the issue. As long as the person visiting the Shrine was a public servant the visit must be seen as official and the act a breach of constitutional law. In fact, the progressives expressed their belief that the Prime Minister and Cabinet members favored visits to Yasukuni because of the privilege associated with gaining entrance into the inner precincts of the Shrine which were closed to members of the general public.[118] This would imply that the conservatives were once again trying to align themselves with a religious organization, thus validating the progressive's accusation of constitutional infringement.

---

including Nakasone, have likened Yasukuni to Arlington Cemetery in Virginia and the Cenotaph in London. However, as Hardacre suggests, there are significant differences between a national memorial cemetery and a religious institution. At Arlington National Cemetery, a cleric of any religion may freely enter and perform an observance or some other rite for the war dead buried there. Yasukuni Shrine is "exclusively a Shinto institution, and it is unthinkable that a cleric of any other religion would perform rites there." For more, see Hardacre, Shinto and the State, 1868-1988, p. 140-142.

[118] *Jurisuto, p. 111.*

The compromise faction entered the debate recommending the creation of a new national memorial devoid of the politico-religious complexities surrounding the Yasukuni Shrine.[119] The new institution would accommodate all Japanese regardless of their religious denomination and mourners would not be forced to use traditional forms of worship because a new memorial would be detached from all religious influences. In the written report, those supporting the compromise did not pursue this option any further because they had not been asked to discuss it by Chief Cabinet Secretary Fujinami.

However, in a commentary by Sono Ayako, a renowned contemporary novelist, it was suggested that the Tomb for Unidentified War Victims at Chidorigafuchi could be considered a replacement for the Yasukuni Shrine. This national memorial was not charged with any religious significance, it was not registered as a religious institution, and anyone could enter and perform observances. According to Sono, Yasukuni was too deeply ensconced in international political debate for it to have a purely national voice.[120] Although she recommended the tomb at Chidorigafuchi for the reasons stated above and

---

[119]   *Jurisuto, p. 113.*

[120]   Sono Ayako. *"Shukyo o tokutei shinai arata na kinenbyo setsuritsu o"* *(Establishing a New Commemoration Memorial that does not Specify Religion). Jurisuto, vol. 848, 1985, p. 32.* Biographical information on Sono Ayako is found in *Gendai Nihon Shippitsusha 77/84 (Biographical Dictionary of Modern Japan). Tokyo: Nichigai Associates, 1984-85.*

because it was a "sacred place with a quiet atmosphere that might remove the [legal and religious] hindrance of Yasukuni from the Prime Minister and Cabinet members," she also felt that the Tomb had been "constructed on such a small scale that many feel it lacks the splendor appropriate to a national memorial."[121]

Interesting in itself was that the compromise faction occupied the last paragraph of the written report. Whether this was because their opinions represented only a minority of those expressed by the Commission or whether the paragraph was placed at the end to suggest a completely new approach for handling the Yasukuni issue is pure conjecture. However, a new national memorial hall to commemorate the Japanese war dead was scheduled for construction by 1995 to mark the fiftieth anniversary of the end of the Pacific War. Managed by the *Nihon Izokukai*, the blueprints originally called for the memorial to be established next to the Yasukuni Shrine, but the government stepped in and delayed its construction due to the influence Yasukuni may have on the display at the new memorial. Furthermore, in what has been called "an extraordinary and unprecedented move," the government changed the original design of the memorial to a peculiar standing S-shape even after all plans had

---

[121] Sono, "Shukyo o tokutei shinai arata na kinenbyo setsuritsu o" *Jurisuto*, p. 31.

been settled. The new memorial continues to be enveloped in controversy with no foreseeable date of completion.[122]

          *   *   *

In assessing the written report, there are several conclusions which can be drawn. It is evident that no solutions were forthcoming for the challenging task of laying the Yasukuni issue to rest. Regardless of the divided report and the Commission's failure to reach a consensus, Nakasone and his cabinet paid formal tribute at Yasukuni on August 15, 1985. This indicates that from the beginning, Nakasone was determined to visit the Shrine but used the Commission as a political front to mask his real intentions. By establishing a commission of prominent members of society and bestowing upon them the power to propose changes in the law, Nakasone made a valiant but flawed attempt to legitimize his actions. His political strategy failed because the members of the Commission represented a cross-section of society that virtually precluded agreement on a unified decision. The Commission brought to the discussions opposing political views that would not prove easily reconciled.

It can also be concluded that the Commission only flushed to the surface opinions representing Japan's pluralistic political culture, encompassing the

---

[122]   *"Cultural Survey, 1994," Monumenta Nipponica, vol. 50, no. 1, (spring 1995): p. 112.*

individual platforms of at least three groups. While Yasukuni was the soapbox upon which Japan's intelligentsia preached, the core issue as to whether the Yasukuni Shrine should continue to be Japan's memorial for the war dead became lost in the shuffle. Yasukuni became a convenient podium where intellectuals have assembled to express their competing desires to fashion postwar identity and restructure postwar nationalism. The issues directly related to the Shrine have thus remained unresolved and the controversy paralyzed. This further suggests the unlikelihood of Yasukuni assuming any postwar significance other than a place where a minority of the population can express nostalgic feelings for a time now past.

In retrospect, the intellectual and political paralysis surrounding Yasukuni may very well have been stimulated initially by the so-called "Shinto directive" and Articles 20 and 89 of Japan's Constitution. However, these orders did not suppress Japanese nationalism, they only fragmented it. The pieces have been picked up by representatives of various political parties who hope to shape the course of Japan's future by realigning Japan's postwar experience with some version of postwar nationalism. Although the occupation authorities administered national policy immediately following Japan's surrender, the task of struggling with the long-term effects of democratization, national reconstruction and identity reformation was, and is, left for the Japanese to contend with. This study suggests that the construction of postwar nationalism will not be monopolized by any particular political party or organization, but will emerge through an amalgamation of different voices which have surfaced since the 1950s.

In my research, I have also found no evidence to support the claim that postwar nationalism exhibits the potential to become the monolithic entity that characterized prewar nationalism. This line of thought seems to have become a convenient obstacle to place before Japanese attempts to reclaim their rights to nation-state issues such as national security. In Japan's contemporary political climate, it is unlikely that any one group will muster enough support to create the ultranationalistic tide that swept over Japan during the war years. If anything, the ideological diversity and contention seen through the prism of the Yasukuni controversy is reflective of Japanese efforts to secure a sense of cultural identity and establish a consensus on the character of postwar nationalism.

Lastly, while debates still linger on the nature of Yasukuni and postwar Japanese nationalism, it can be concluded that Yasukuni was successfully transported into the postwar era by the Japanese, although the impetus may have very well derived from SCAP officials. The progressives see Yasukuni as unnecessary baggage and an impediment to the process of change, the fulcrum of their political agenda. The conservatives perceive Yasukuni as a pillar of the nation, and the compromise faction believes the Shrine should just be left alone.

But where are the voices of the ordinary people and what position do they take

on the Yasukuni Shrine issue?

Chapter IV   Nationalism versus Internationalism

Both proponents and opponents of the movement to re-establish state patronage of the Yasukuni Shrine are under the impression that this issue occupies the minds of the average Japanese citizen. Quite the contrary seems true, however. Beyond the conservative, progressive and compromise positions articulated in the Hayashi Commission's report, a 4th strain of thought on the Yasukuni issue - - which will be referred to here as the "silent majority" - - can be detected. This group represents those voices which have gone virtually unheard in this debate. They represent the segment of the Japanese population that has either been excluded from this politco-religious discourse, other than through opinion polls, or has displayed a general disinterest in the fate of Yasukuni.

One explanation for why the general population has been absent from the Yasukuni debate and, by extension, the defining processes of postwar nationalism, is because Japanese intellectuals have dominated the postwar political scene, leaving little if any room for popular participation. In his "Commentary on Nationalism in Japan: Nationalism as Intellectual History," the historian Harry Harootunian suggests that,

> Nationalism in the postwar is defined by the fears and anxieties of
> intellectuals who achieved maturity before the war and who kept
> close vigil on its location since 1945 . . . this fear of nationalism
> stems from social categories of analysis which were once relevant

to a society in process of modernizing but which today are useless in understanding the kind of society Japanese have constructed since the war. This fear is also informed by a curious conception of history which sees the past recurring in the present, even though the present is different from the past.[123]

The fear within Japan of history repeating itself may no longer be valid, but the possibility is kept very much alive by intellectuals who monitor the character of contemporary nationalism by continuously addressing it and comparing it to prewar nationalism. This, in turn, has accentuated prewar nationalism and thwarted Japan's ability to move forward with any concrete notion of postwar nationalism unpoliced by the Japanese themselves. The very act of believing that the past could re-occur has prevented present notions of nationalism from progressing and evolving. Fears and anxieties of ultranationalism, militarism and aggression might very well dissipate if they were not continuously brought back into public consciousness. The paradox, of course, is that this kind of history should not be forgotten in order to prevent it from re-occurring again.

Despite the overwhelming predominance of intellectual commentary and international criticism on the Yasukuni issue, the "silent majority" *has* had a voice, one which, in the end, may reverberate louder than the others. Having studied contemporary middle-class society, Murakami Yasusuke described the

---

[123] Harootunian, Harry D. *"Commentary on Nationalism in Japan: Nationalism as Intellectual History." Journal of Asian Studies*, vol. 31, no. 5 (1971): 62.

postwar generation's position on traditional symbols of nationalism as one of indifference: "Public opinion polls indicate that the new middle mass has little motivation for recreating a Japanese identity centered around any traditional symbol. This is especially true of the younger generation . . . ."[124] Taking the voice of the masses one step further, William Chapman stated that young and middle-aged Japanese in the 1980s believed "Yasukuni Shrine was merely a fine place to drink oneself silly under the cherry trees in April . . . . The notion that Yasukuni was a burning national issue was a fiction nursed by the press and professional leftists and rightists in Japan."[125]

Indeed, a public opinion poll printed in the _Yomiuri Shimbun_ on August 10, 1985 revealed that 72% of the 3000 respondents displayed a general interest in the Shrine in so far as it was important to consoling bereaved family members. The public believed it "proper" for the state to conduct ceremonies to console the spirits of those who died for their country. The predominant feeling expressed by the public, therefore, was one of sympathy for the bereaved families rather than support for the Yasukuni Shrine as a symbol of Japanese identity and nationalism.[126]

---

[124] Murakami, Yasusuke, "'New Middle Mass' Japanese: Where do we go from here?" _Look Japan_, January 10, 1985.

[125] Chapman, "Inventing Japan," pp. 253 and 232

[126] "Senso taiken, kempo kenkaku o hanei," (War Experience, Reflecting

The emergence of the silent majority in postwar Japan and Japanese historiography symbolizes a drastic change in Japanese society after the 1945 defeat and the Occupation. They have surfaced as a powerful group to participate in the dialogue between the conservatives, progressives and compromise faction. The silent majority represents a formidable voice because, having been suppressed in prewar Japan by censorship laws, state-policing and threats of social castigation, they are now free to express their opinions in a public forum and help determine the course of domestic events. Having been liberated from a class historically referred to as the *helpless common people*, the silent majority counter the LDP's desire to employ Yasukuni as a political tool and infuse the nation with a sense of nationalism from above. In one sense, the silent majority has become the constable of postwar Japanese democracy, securing for themselves a right to public policy making over national concerns, especially those related to the preservation of peace.

*   *   *

As expressed in Chapter I, concern over the past re-emerging in the present has also been promoted by foreign countries exploited by Japan during World War II. China and Korea refuse to allow the diminishment of national and international public memory of wartime atrocities and the symbols of Japan's

---

Constitutional Feelings). Yomiuri Shimbun, 1985, p. 4.

international aggression. In 1996, almost eleven years after Nakasone visited the Yasukuni Shrine, Prime Minister Hashimoto Ryutaro along with six Cabinet members paid an official visit to the Shrine. When asked by the Kyodo News about his visit and the potential criticism it would raise, Hashimoto confidently stated, "Why should it matter any more? It's time to stop letting that sort of thing complicate our international relations."[127]

The Korean Times criticized Hashimoto's actions, stating that official visits defied "critics of Japanese historical amnesia and those who argue that such visits are unconstitutional."[128] At the same time, a China Daily commentary printed on August 15, 1996 responded strongly to Hashimoto's visit. The author stated that Hashimoto set an example that "could lead to a militaristic revival in Japan. All these events [eliminating wartime history from the textbooks, politicians denying Japanese aggression during World War II, and visiting the Yasukuni Shrine], in whatever guise they may appear, are pro-militaristic in nature." The editorial goes on to say that the Japanese have "posed a challenge to the stability of Asia and the world."[129] These international confrontations

---

[127]   "Japan Premier Visits Shrine to War Dead," The New York Times. 29 July 1996.

[128]   "Japan Ministers Visit Controversial War Shrine," The Korean Times. 16 August 1996.

[129]   "Japan at Crossroad," China Daily. 15 August 1996.

support my conclusion that the Yasukuni Shrine is no longer Japan's possession. It has been globally expropriated and internationalized through history and debate.

The Yasukuni controversy continues partially due to global fears of a nascent Japanese militarism and resurrection of the lingering negative impressions, images and memories of a fanatically imperialistic nation. Surely the Japanese are aware of this. But they must also be cognizant of the fact that attempts to remarry the state with religion, as such a bonding would symbolize, could be more detrimental than allowing the controversy to continue. In the light of Japan's global economic status, specifically during the 1980s, why would the Japanese risk promoting Japanese nationalism through the use of so sensitive an institution as the Yasukuni Shrine? How could Japan make that move without prompting damaging effects? Why would Japan risk jeopardizing or even losing the leadership status and privileged position it has sewn for herself? These questions still occupy the periphery of the Yasukuni Shrine controversy but they are pulsing toward the center ever so subtlely. Perhaps this is one reason why the Yasukuni Shrine has remained on the shelf through most of the postwar period, blending in with the many other complex issues facing contemporary Japanese society.

Since 1985, the Yasukuni Shrine problem has surfaced on cue, on every

August 15th. This is because other nations consider it a convenient time to exact war reparations from Japan either in the form of public apology or monetary amends. But between these overt controversies, the Shrine has also become inextricably intertwined with a host of broader international concerns. This leads to the conclusion that the original controversy may simply have been an outgrowth of more pressing postwar global issues. For example, among the noteworthy national and international questions facing Japan over the last decade are the following:

- Should Japanese Self-Defense Forces be allowed to join United Nations peacekeeping operations in the Persian Gulf? Should Japan be allowed to send any troops if the international situation warrants it? How can Japan send troops if the Constitution prohibits it? Should Japan revise its Constitution? How can Japan revise its Constitution if it was written and imposed by the United States? If Japan is an independent nation, why do the Japanese not revise their own Constitution?

- What does Japan do with the Japanese soldiers killed in the line of duty? Would they be enshrined in Yasukuni or receive burial rites according to the wishes of the family? If they are enshrined in Yasukuni, as Yasukuni officials claim the right to do since these soldiers died in service to their country, what legal recourse do the families of these soldiers have if they do not want their loved ones enshrined due in large part to their right to freedom of religion? If the Constitution forbids Yasukuni to enshrine soldiers, since it is a matter of the state, why is Yasukuni enshrining soldiers?[130]

- If the Japanese no longer harbor intentions of reviving militarism and aggression, why are the country's leaders going to Yasukuni? Why do the leaders commemorate the end of World War II and their commitment to peace by paying reverence to the war dead? Why do the Japanese not apologize for their active role during World War II? Why does the international community annually criticize Japan on August 15 and

---

[130] *For more information on the legality vs. illegality of enshrinements, contradictions in the separation of religion and state, freedom of religion, and postwar constitutional problems, see Norma Field's, In the Realm of the Dying Emperor, Chapter II entitled: "Yamaguchi: An Ordinary Woman" (p. 107-174), is a narrative description of one woman's legal battle with the Japanese judicial system to have her husband's name removed from the Yamaguchi Defense-of-the-Nation Shrine. The husband was killed in 1968 in a traffic accident while on the job as a member of the Self-Defense Force. Several years later, her husband was enshrined as a diety to "safeguard" the nation. The widow was a Christian and subsequently charged the Yamaguchi Veterans Association and Self-Defense Force of Yamaguchi prefecture with violation of the constitutional provisions for the separation of religion and state as well as violation of her religious rights. Fifteen years later, the Supreme Court ruled in favor of the defendants.*

83

mention their concern over the revival of militarism and aggression if the Japanese Constitution forbids it?

The Yasukuni Shrine, or more to the point, the symbolic residue and resonance of Yasukuni, has become enmired in a host of directly and indirectly related issues as Japan, the other nations of East Asia, and the rest of the world sort out the lingering aftermath of World War II. One can liken Yasukuni to that of a shadow that has been cast on many aspects of society, nations and debates, yet which remains mysterious, moving and intangible. Whether or not the Japanese believe Yasukuni is important in their daily lives, the fact remains that the Shrine, along with the plethora of questions it raises, *does* have an abiding impact socially, economically,   politically, and intellectually.   The Shrine exists, possesses a long heritage, and has a following.

*   *   *

From the moment the *Nihon Izokukai* first pressed for the re-nationalization of the Yasukuni Shrine, the state has endeavored to use it to further its own ends. However, this effort has not proven successful because societal perceptions and understanding of the Shrine remain very divided. The nature of postwar nationalism, however, represents a slightly more complicated problem. After 1945, prewar nationalism was discredited and subsumed. As the postwar progressed, new notions of nationalism evolved centered primarily on ideas of economic growth and advancement. Yet the ghost of prewar nationalism has continued to haunt contemporary discussions of the subject. Although most people -- such as the silent majority -- have tried to ignore this phantom of the past, others have attempted to use it to further their political agendas. Conservatives like Nakasone have tried to revive some of the prewar nationalist spirit, both directly through the rehabilitation of the Shrine and indirectly through *kokusaika*. Meanwhile, progressives and Asian nations have used Yasukuni as a lever for attacking conservative issues like remilitarization. The result is that the shape of Japanese nationalism remains an unsettled issue. Yasukuni is always present, but it only seems to offer more complications, not solutions.

The Yasukuni Shrine is an unclosed chapter of postwar Japanese history. The Shrine remains an issue due to its past and present historical significance. It has continuing relevance as a vehicle of nationalistic dissemination between the Japanese government and the people, and it continues to have an impact as a national and international symbol of war-time memories. It is a lingering remnant of unhealed wounds at the core of Japan's contemporary identity in the world.

The Shrine also stands as an icon of an antiquated system no longer suitable to Japan ideologically or symbolically. Yet, it has provided Japanese postwar intellectuals and numerous other voices with a discursive space in which to communicate, and an anvil on which to potentially forge a new identity and nationalism for the Japanese. With this in mind, perhaps when, and if, the controversy is finally put to rest, Yasukuni too will assume a new postwar image reflective of the democratic ideals put forth during the occupation and the traditional values underlying the nation. One can only hope that the Shrine will be instrumental in helping the Japanese merge their past and present histories in order to construct a better future.

Appendix A

The following is a list of the 15 members of the hayashi Commission and their respective titles:

1. Hayashi Keizo President of the Japan Red Cross Society

2. Ashibe Nobuyoshi   Gakushuin University Professor

3. Umehara Takeshi   Kyoto Shiritsu Geijutsu University President

4. Eto Jun   Prominent Public Intellectual

5. Oguchi Iichi   Tokyo University Honorary Professor

6. Kojima Kazushi   Tohoku University Professor

7. Sato Isao   Tokai University Professor

8. Suetsugu Ichiro   Zaidan Hojin Ikusei Kyokai Riji (Director of Youth

        Organization)

9. Suzuki Haruo Owner of Showa Electric Company

10. Sono Ayako   Renowned Contemporary Novelist

11. Tagami Jyoji   Osaka University Honorary Professor

12. Chino Taraou Former General Secretary to the Diet

13. Nakamura Hajime   Tokyo University Honorary Professor

14. Hayashi Shuzo   Former Cabinet Member and Chairman of this Commission

15. Yokoi Daizo   Lawyer

Bibliography

Japanese Sources

Gendai Nihon shippitsusha daijiten 77/84 (Biographical Dictionary of Modern Japan). Tokyo: Nichigai Associates, 1984-85.

Hashimoto Kiminobu. "Seikyo bunri to Yasukuni hokokusho" (Report of Yasukuni and the Separation of State and Religion). Jurisuto, vol. 848, 1985: 48-53.

Hijikata Yoshio. Yasukuni Jinja kokka shinto wa yomigaeru ka! (Is the Yasukuni Shrine and State Shinto Being Resurrected?). Tokyo: Shakai Hyoronsha, 1985.

"Kakuryo no Yasukuni Jinja sanpai mondai ni kan suru kondankai hokokusho" (Report of the roundtable on the issue of Official Visits to Yasukuni Shrine by Cabinet Members). Jurisuto, vol. 848, 1985: 110-113.

"Kakuryo no Yasukuni Jinja sanpai de kondankai'" (Roundtable Discussion on Official Visits to the Yasukuni Shrine by Cabinet Members). Asahi Nenkan, 1985.

Oe Shinobu. Yasukuni jinja mondai (The Yasukuni Shrine Problem). Tokyo: Iwanami shoten, 1984.

"Senso taiken, kempo kenkaku o hanei," (War Experience, Reflecting Constitutional Feelings). Yomiuri Shimbun, 7 August 1985.

Shuzo Hayashi. "Kakuryo no Yasukuni Jinja sanpai mondai kodankai no ho kokusho ni tsuite" (Regarding the Report of the Roundtable on the issue of Official Visits to Yasukuni Shrine by Cabinet Members). Jurisuto, vol. 848, 1985: 40-44.

Sawafuji Toichiro. Iwate Yasukuni iken sosho, (Opinion on the Lawsuit between Yasukuni and Iwate Prefecture). Shin Nihon Shuppansha, 1992.

Shintei gendai Nihon jinmeiroku (New Edition of Modern Japanese Names and Bibliographies). Tokyo: Nichigai Associates, 1994.
Sono Ayako. "Shukyo o tokutei shinai arata na kinenbyo setsuritsu o" (Establishing a New Commemoration Memorial that does not Specify Religion). Jurisuto, vol. 848, 1985: 32-33.

English - Language Sources

Brown, Delmer M. Nationalism in Japan: An Introductory Historical Analysis. Berkeley: University of California Press, 1955.

Buruma, Ian. The Wages of Guilt: Memories of War in Germany and Japan. New York: Harper Collins, 1994.

Chapman, William. Inventing Japan: The Making of a Postwar Civilization. New York: Prentice Hall Press, 1991.

Creemers, Wilhelmus H. M. Shrine Shinto after World War II. Leiden, Netherlands: E.J. Brill, 1968.

"Cultural Survey, 1994." Monumenta Nipponica, vol. 50, no. 1 (Spring 1994): 103-116.

Duara, Prasenjit. Rescuing History from the Nation. Chicago: The University of Chicago press, 1995.

Fane, Richard A. B. Ponsonby. The Vicissitudes of Shinto. Kakikamo, Kyoto: The Ponsonby Memorial Society, 1963.

Field, Norma. In the Realm of the Dying Emperor. New York: Pantheon Books, 1991.

Fukatsu Masumi. "A State Visit to Yasukuni Shrine." Japan Quarterly, vol. 33, no. 1 (1986) 19-24.

Gluck, Carol. Japan's Modern Myths: Ideology in the Late Meiji Period.

Princeton: Princeton University Press, 1985.

_____. "The Past in the Present." In Postwar Japan as History, ed. Andrew Gordon. 64-95. Berkeley: University of California Press, 1993.

John Goodman and Kirsten Refsing. Ideology and Practice in Modern Japan. New York: Routledge, 1992.

Hardacre, Helen. Shinto and the State: 1868-1988. Princeton: Princeton University Press, 1989.

Harootunian, Harry D. "Commentary on Nationalism in Japan: Nationalism as Intellectual History." Journal of Asian Studies, vol. 31, no. 5 (1971): 57-62.

Holtom, D.C. Modern Japan and Shinto Nationalism. 1947; rpt. New York: Paragon Book Reprint Corporation, 1963.

Irokawa Daikichi. The Culture of the Meiji Period. Princeton: Princeton University Press, 1985.

Kitagawa, Joseph M. Religion in Japanese History. New York: Columbia University press, 1990.

Kodansha Encyclopedia of Japan. Tokyo: Kodansha Ltd., 1993, S.v. "Liberal Democratic Party," by Haruhiro Fukui.

Koschmann, Victor J. "Intellectuals and Politics." in Postwar Japan as History, ed. Andrew Gordon. Berkeley: University of California Press, 1993.

_____. The Mito Ideology: Discourse, Reform and Insurrection in Late Tokugawa Japan, 1790-1864. Berkeley: University of California Press, 1987.

Kohn, Hans. Nationalism: Its Meaning and History. Princeton: D. Van Nostrand Company, INC., 1955.

Maruyama, Masao. Thought and Behavior in Modern Japanese Politics. ed. Ivan Morris. London: Oxford University Press, 1963.

Murakami, Yasusuke. "'New Middle Mass' Japanese: Where do we go from here?" Look Japan, January 10, 1985.

Nakasone, Yasuhiro. My Life in Politics. (Nat Sayer, Trans.) Draft.

Olson, Lawrence. Ambivalent Moderns: Portaraits of Japanese Cultural Identity. Rowman and Littlefield Publishers, Inc., 1982.

Pyle, Kenneth B. The Japanese Question: Power and Purpose in a New Era. Washington, D.C.: The AEI Press, 1992.

_____. "The Future of Japanese Nationality: An Essay in Contemporary History." Journal of Japanese Studies, vol.8, no. 2 (1982): 223-263.

_____. "In Pursuit of a Grand Design: Nakasone Betwixt the Past and the Future." Journal of Japanese Studies, vol. 13, no. 2 (1987): 243-270.

_____. "A Symposium on Japanese Nationalism: Some Recent Approaches to Japanese Nationalism." Journal of Asian Studies, vol. 31, no. 5 (1971): 5-16.

_____. "The Japanese Self-Image." Journal of Japanese Studies, vol. 5, no. 1 (1979): 1-4.

_____. "The Technology of Japanese Nationalism: The Local Improvement Movement, 1900-1918," Journal of Asian Studies. 33, no. 1 (1973): 51-65.

Robert E. Ward and Frank Joseph Shulman. The Allied Occupation of Japan, 1945-1952: An Annotated Bibliography of Western Language Materials. Chicago: The American Library Association, 1974.

Sakai, Takeshi. "A Matter of Faith." Japan Quarterly, vol. 35, no. 4 (1988) 357-364.

Vlastos, Steven. Peasant Protests and Uprisings in Tokugawa Japan. Berkeley: The University of California Press, 1986.

Woodard, William P. The Allied Occupation of Japan 1945 - 1952 and Japanese Religions. Leiden: E. J. Brill, 1972.

91

_____. "Yasukuni Shrine," Japan Christian Quarterly. 37 (Spring 1971): 72-9.

Newspaper and Magazine Articles

"A New Japanese Nationalism," The New York Times, 12 April 1987.

"An Aspect of Nakasone's Politics," The Japan Times, 23 August 1985.

"Fury Over Nakasone Tribute to War Dead," The London Times, 16 August 1985.

"Hirohito: Criminal or Puppet?" U.S. News & World Report, 17 March 1950.

"Japan at Crossroad," China Daily, 15 August 1996.

"Japan Ministers Visit Controversial War Shrine," Korean Times, 16 August 1996

"Nakasone Calls off Shrine Trip," The Japan Times, 15 August 1986.

"Nakasone's Shrine Visit Draws Fire," Beijing Review, 7 September 1985.

"Our Internationalization or Yours?," The Japan Times, 22 September 1988.

"Official Yasukuni Visits May Be Allowable: Advisory Panel," The Japan Times International Edition, 10 August 1985.

"Prime Minister's Visit to Yasukuni," The Japan Times Weekly, International Edition, 26 August 1978.

"Suzuki, Ministers Defy Critics, Pay Homage at Yasukuni Shrine," The Japan Times Weekly, International Edition, 16 August 1982.

"The Yasukuni Issue: Christian Prime Minister's Visit to Shrine Stirs

Controversy," The Japan Times Weekly, International Edition, 5 May 1979.

"Tokyo 40 Years Later: War Dead are Honored," The New York Times, 16 August 1985.

"Worshippers Favor Visits by Officials," The Japan Times, 16 August 1992.

"Yasukuni Shrine Debate Begins," The Japan Times Weekly, International Edition, 19 August 1984.

"Yasukuni Shrine Reform Remains Hot Live Issue," The Japan Times Weekly, 11 May 1974.

"Yasukuni In New Dress," Japan Christian Activity News, 10 February 1972.

Undergraduate Honors Thesis

Chandler, Clayton. "Meet Me At Yasukuni! Postwar Japanese Nationalism and the Shrine of the 'Tranquil Land'." Undergraduate Honors Thesis, Harvard University, 1985.

Printed in the United States
63847LVS00003B/13-60